ENZO MICCIO

Italian Dream Wedding

MONDADORI

Each new book is a source of endless joy, the joy of looking back at all the hard work that went into making dreams come true.
This book is dedicated to all the couples who trusted me to organize the most important day of their lives.

"Beauty is nothing other than the promise of happiness"
(Stendhal, *L'amour*)

Beauty is harmony, a perfect equilibrium between the various elements of a magic melody. It is resplendent, emotional, and wonderful; it lifts the spirit and turns joy into a tangible reality. It is hard to describe, a dream come true, something I find in every detail of daily life, in the arts, in nature. It only reveals its full power to those who have eyes to see.

Beauty is that imperceptible smile between two lovers, a guest's furtive tear of joy, the sheer happiness of a bride. It is a fleeting moment that can only fill your heart with true serenity.

Wedding planning is about creating beauty; a successful wedding is a tapestry of individual elements woven into the perfect pattern, embodying precisely the right atmosphere and the right mood. When I create a wedding, I visualize the exact setting and each single moment. I draw inspiration from the location and design the spaces to ensure the perfect dynamics for the event.

My beauty is a timeless dream, scented with the perfume of rare blooms, stretching into landscapes etched in my heart. It gleams in a glance exchanged between two lovers who have decided to write the story of the rest of their lives on a single page, a love story that deserves the right narrative.

Enzo Miccio

Contents

An Enchanted Garden

Annarita and Mario are celebrating their wedding beneath the frescoed vaults of Acireale's majestic cathedral in Sicily. The historic building is flooded with the intensely luminous colors of May. The magnificent church has been transformed into an airy Italian garden as a simple counterpoint to its own rich colors, reflecting the fertile spring burgeoning beyond its doors. White and green predominate; the aisle is strewn with white petals and lined with bright green boxwood parterres, while trees of boxwood and hydrangea, roses and white peonies romantically alternate to mark the pews. The parterres are edged in white polyanthus roses and the arches separating the aisles are highlighted with bright green leafy camphor cones.

The bride's bouquet reflects the dominating motif used to decorate the cathedral: simple white sweet peas, disarming in their fragility, with scalloped edges reminiscent of impalpable organza. The youthful bridesmaids, gravely concentrated on their task as ring bearers, wear white with touches of green too, one of them carrying a bespoke cushion of Sicilian lace, a traditional local handicraft, bearing the precious rings.

The bride's ball gown dress is fit for a princess: in silk Mikado, it is set off by a stunning veil embroidered with petals, echoing the petals on the bodice. Annarita's thick hair is cleverly confined into an elaborate coil held in place by a family heirloom tiara.

The conservatory attached to the family villa has been transformed into a *jardin d'hiver* where native Mediterranean species mix with tropical plants. White and green leaves do duty as menus, while the tables are decorated exclusively with peonies in every imaginable shade of pink, the same blooms adorning the arches framing the cutting of a magnificent cake for the 300 guests.

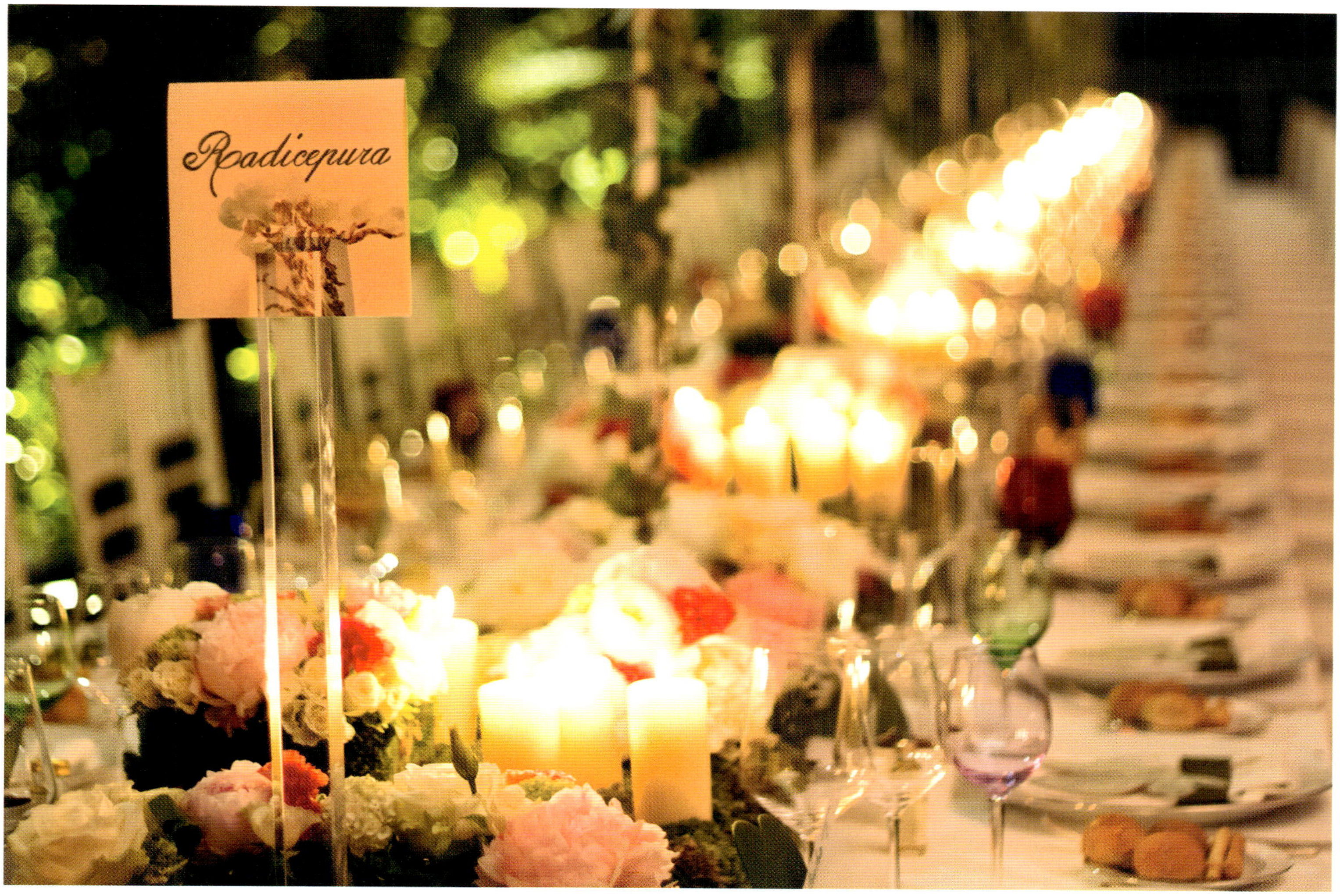
Radicepura

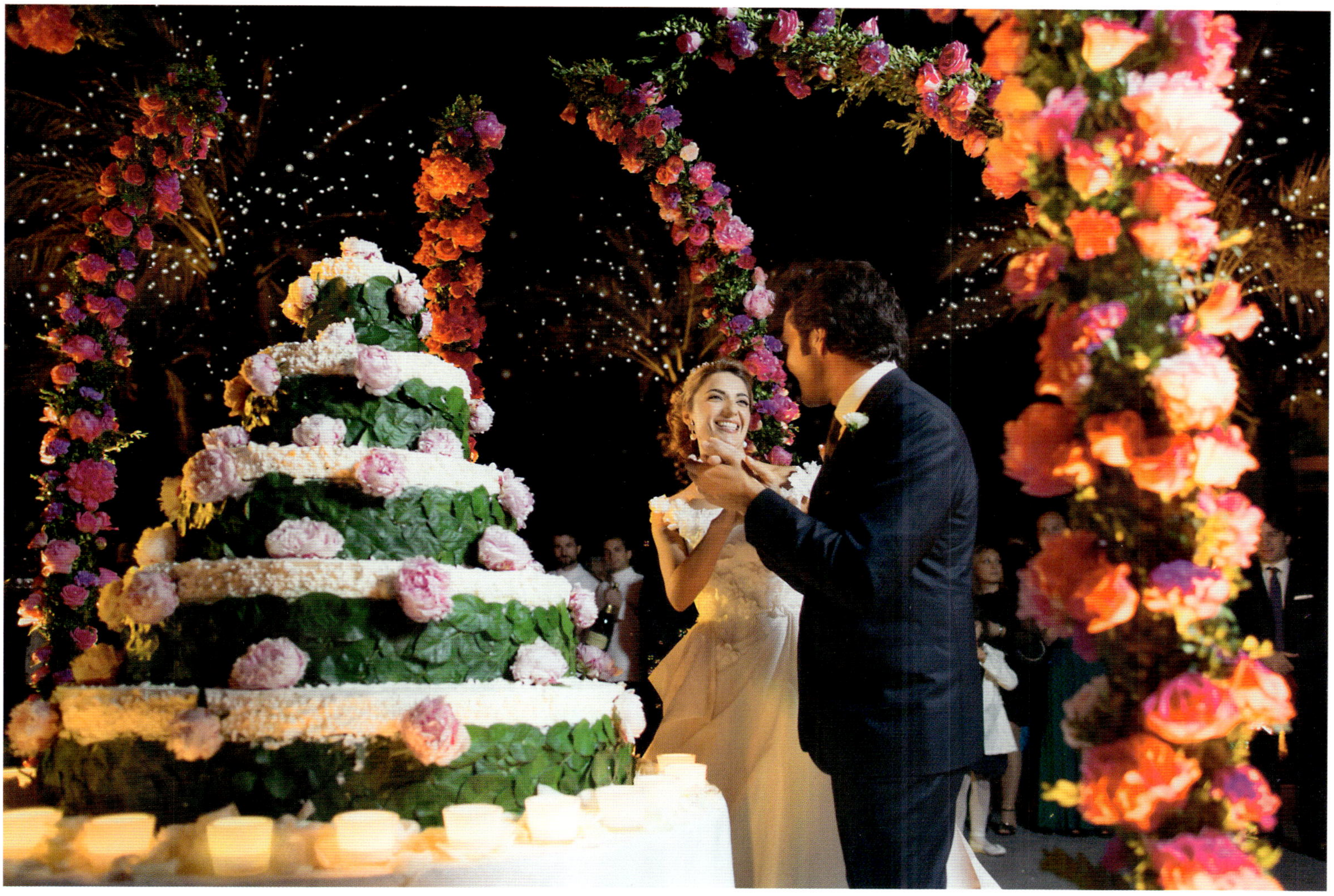

The Lady of the Lake

Months of preparation, painstaking attention to every single detail and perfect logistics led up to this spectacular wedding on a tiny exclusive island on Lake Garda for a bride and groom from abroad who both adore Italy. Guests flooding in from all over Europe are overwhelmed by the sheer beauty of the location.

The ceremony is held on the broad terrace of a Neo-Gothic Venetian-style villa overlooking the lake, with terraces and Italian gardens sloping down to its shores. All set in lush grounds abounding in native flora, exotic imports and rare essences, with unique blooms entwined around the columns of the terrace to create a slice of bridal heaven. The wedding takes place on 11 July at sunset and both the bride's and bridesmaids' dresses reflect the evening mood. By a curious coincidence the bride finds an old calendar in her room displaying the very same date as her own wedding. She wears a figure-hugging gown with an elaborate silk gazar skirt, less delicate, but as airy and transparent as organza. The bridesmaids wear old rose embellished with embroidered sequins.

Roses, lisianthuses, dahlias and white and dusky pink hydrangeas are gathered in soft garlands on the eight imperial tables for the wedding guests in a huge marquee in the garden. The same flower arrangements bedeck the various gazebos with comfortable sofas and provide a romantic setting for the cutting of the cake, with an intricate pattern of different icings personalizing each layer. Simply chic.

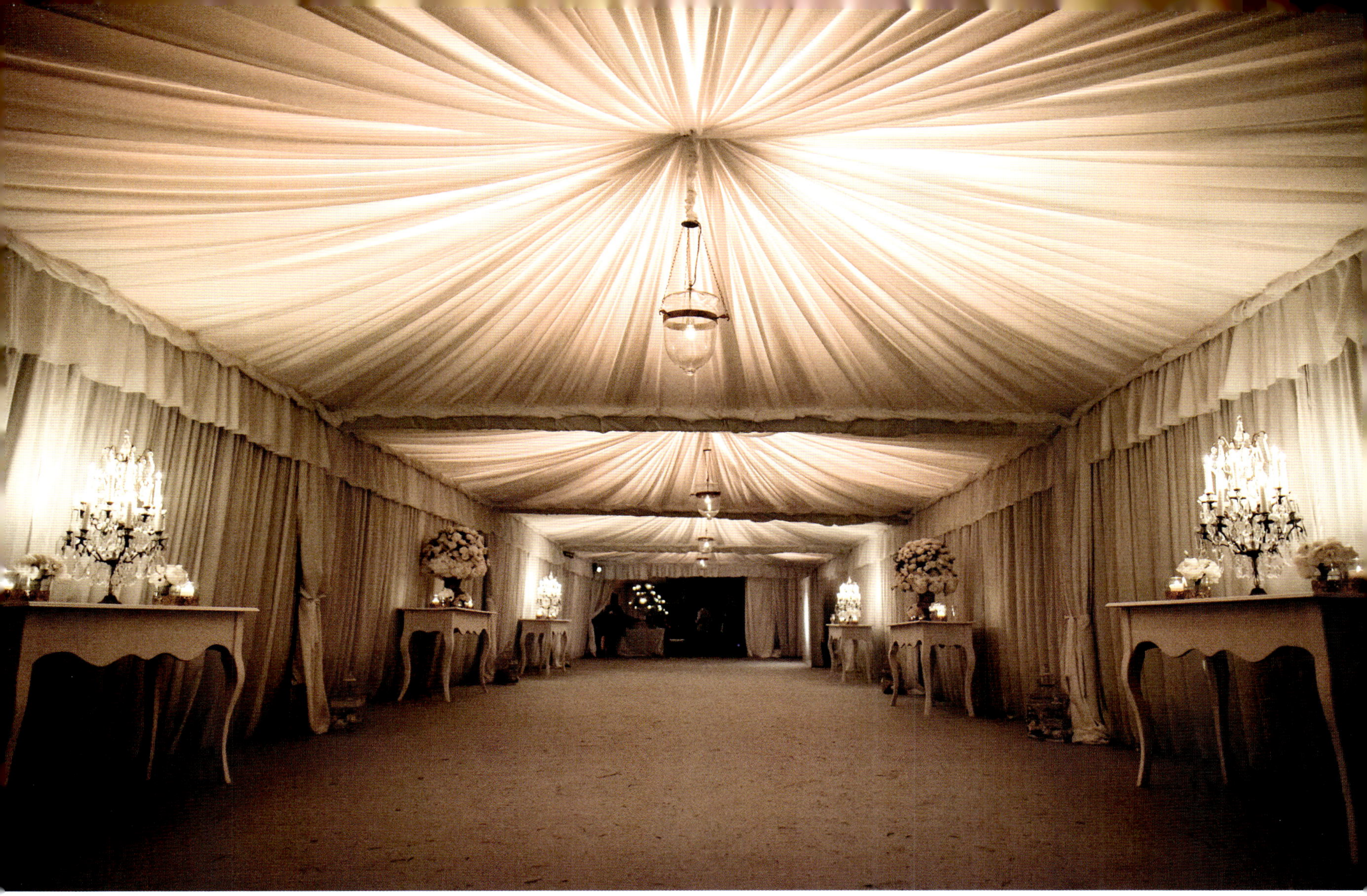

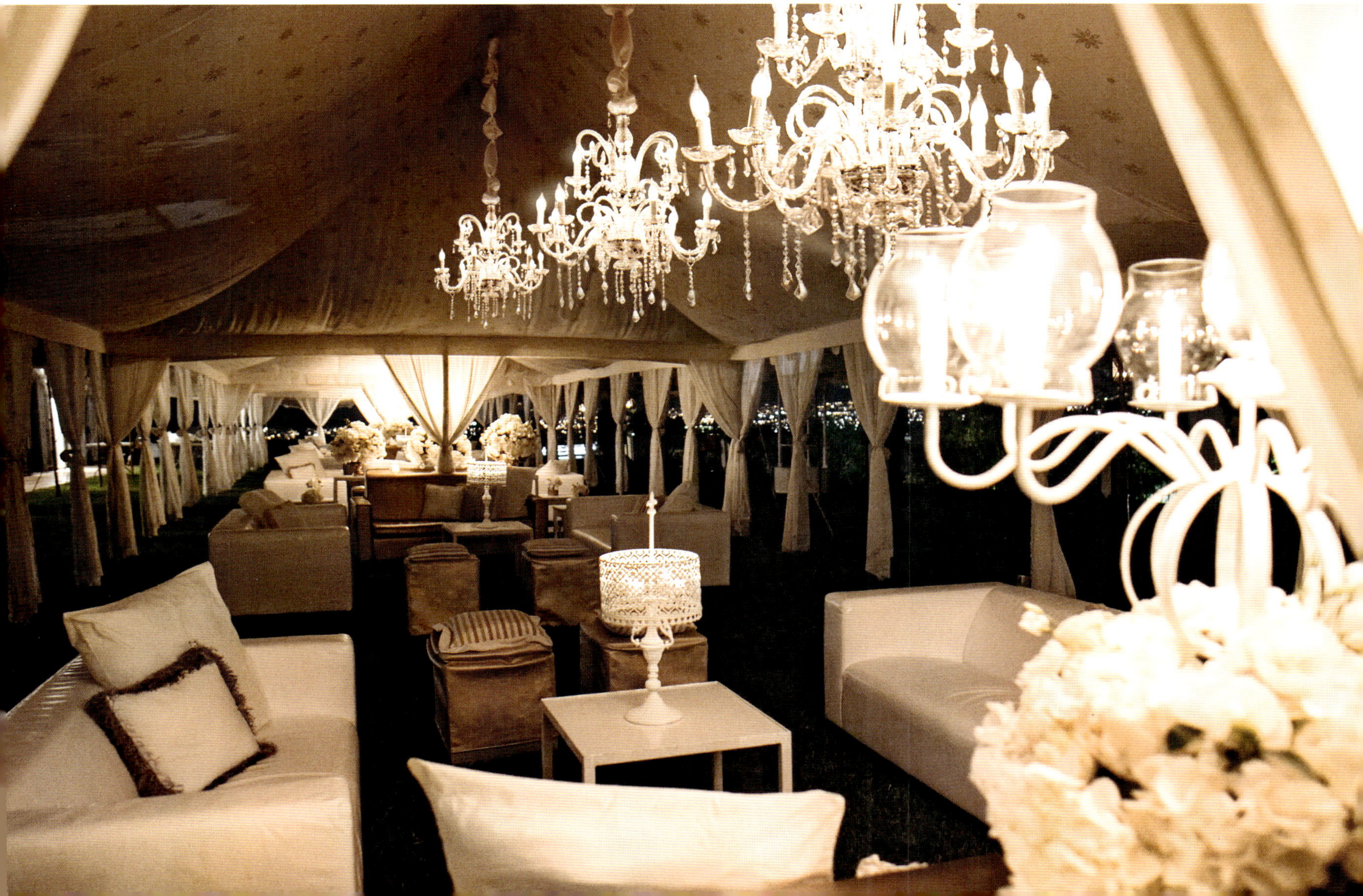

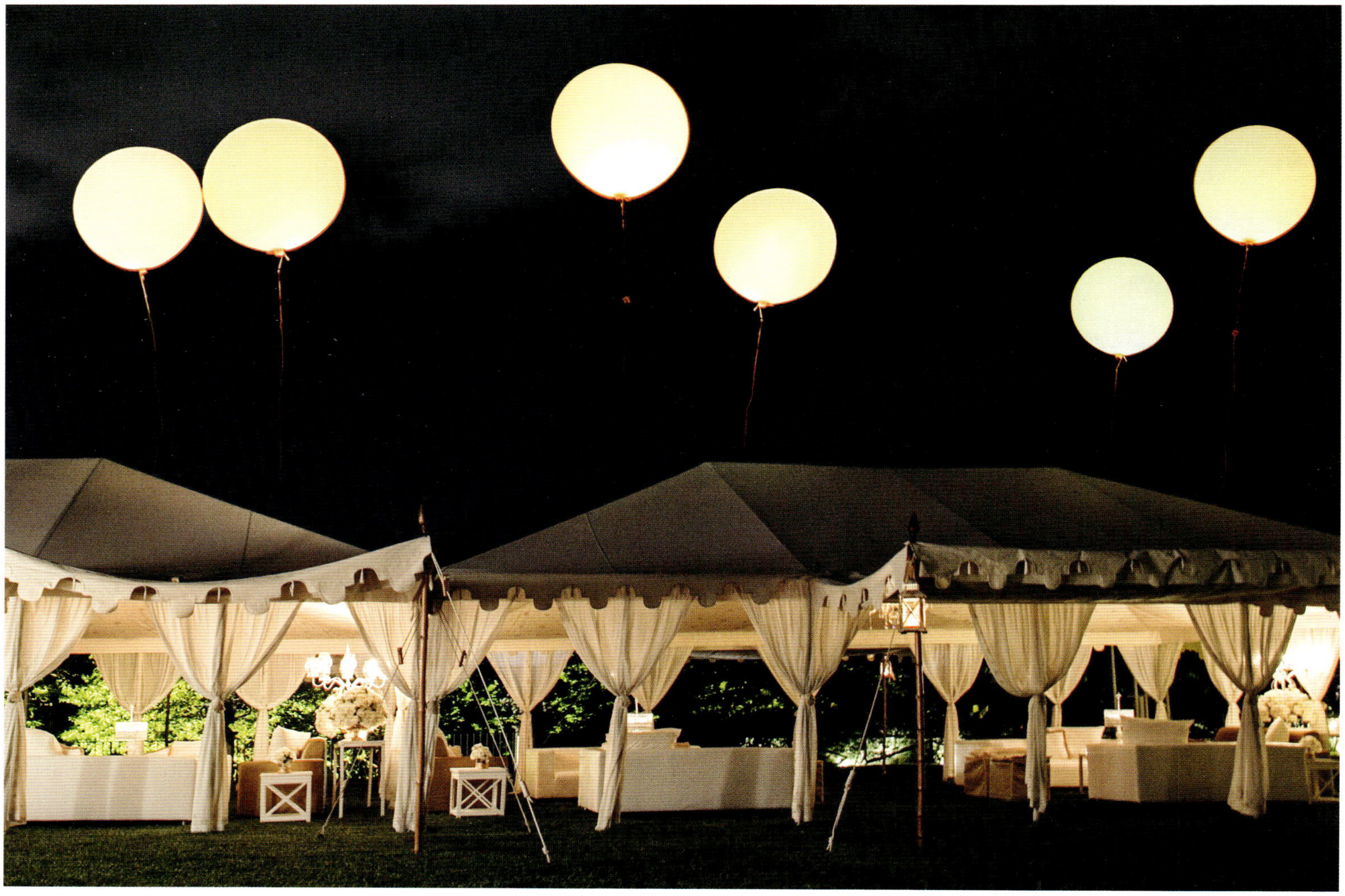

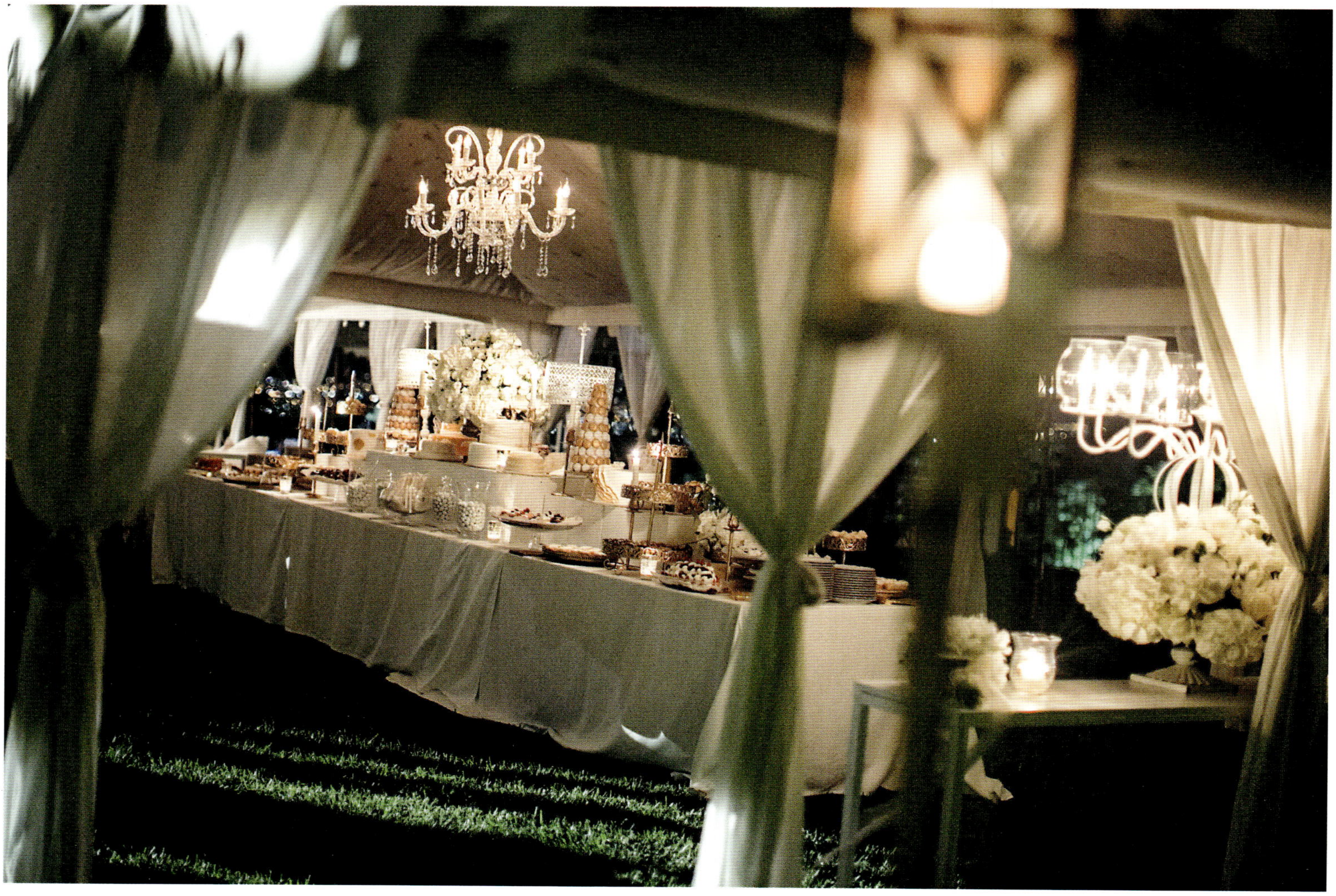

Folklore
on Colorful Capri

Sunlit Capri proved the perfect setting for a round of stunning parties in the days leading up to this wedding. Guests were entertained at a white party, a barbecue party and on a boat trip to explore the crystal seas, bays and grottoes of this magical island in the Bay of Naples. After the wedding in church, the bridal couple were greeted by adorable flower girls and escorted by a colorful local band with their guests to enjoy drinks, music and traditional dances in Capri's famous *piazzetta*.

This convivial prelude was followed by the reception on a terrace overlooking an enchanting bay in a private villa. Capri was once the favorite retreat of the Roman emperors, the playground of the gods, and the sumptuous white and gold of the table settings held a hint of imperial splendor. The delicate white flower arrangements set off the gold tableware to perfection, highlighting the gold decorations handcrafted for the occasion, while the bride and groom's initials embroidered on the napkins provided a final golden touch. The menu? Seafood and fish recipes according to the cream of Capri's renowned culinary tradition.

*Garlands of simple white
flowers adorn the altar
in the 17th-century church
of Santo Stefano overlooking
the famous piazzetta
where the bride threw
her bouquet.*

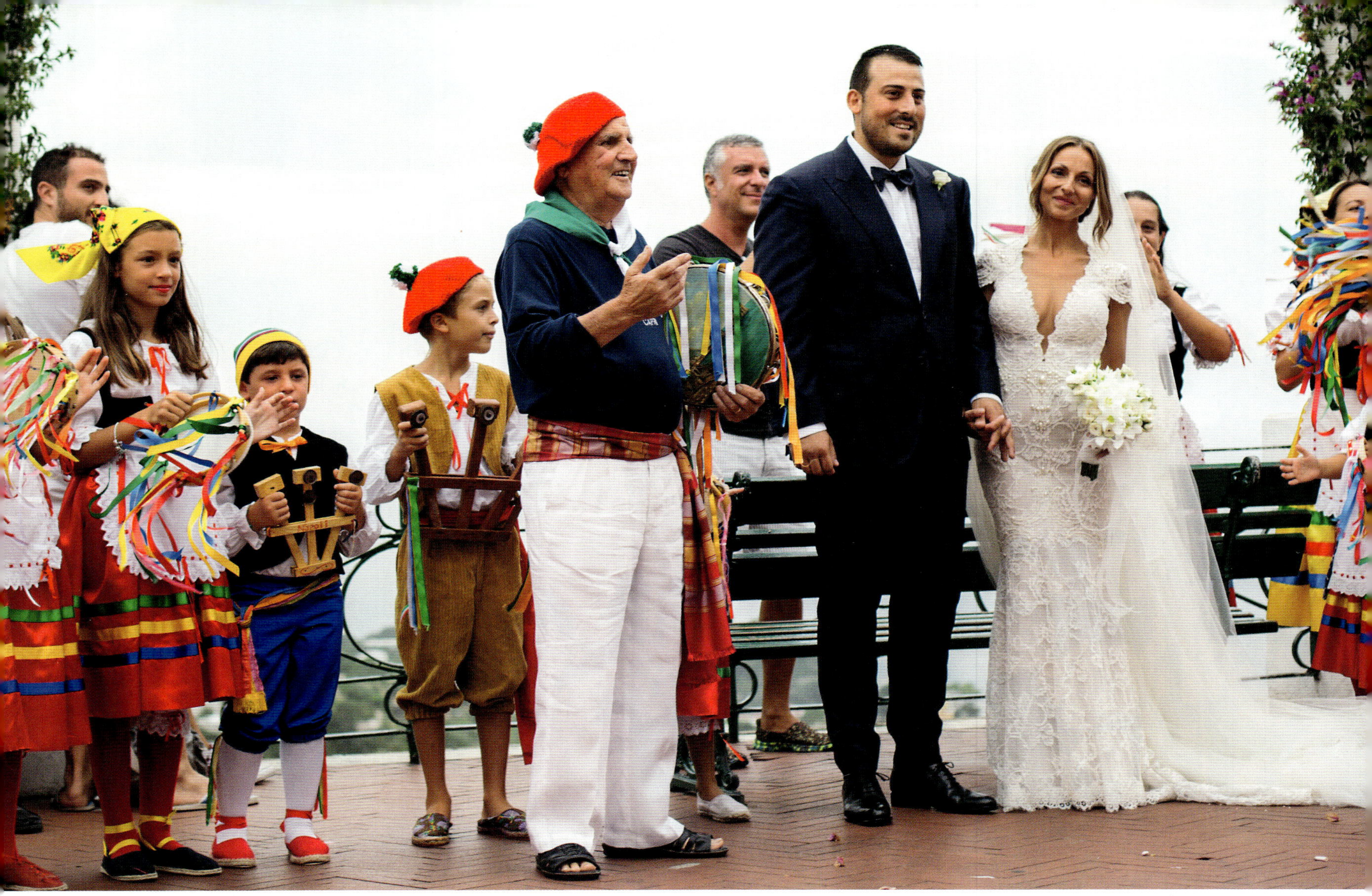

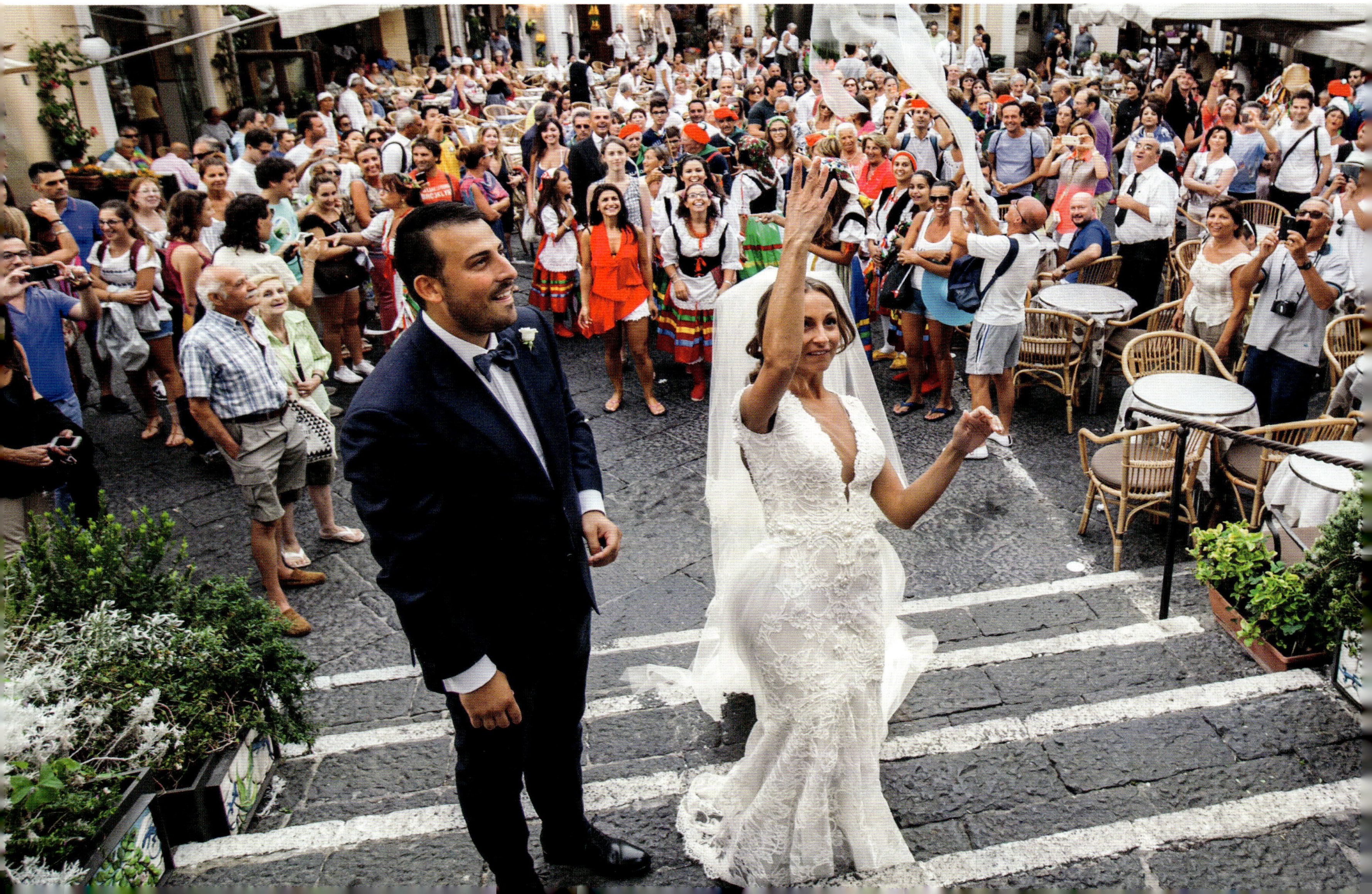

*Part of the villa's tree-shaded
garden was illuminated
by romantic hanging lamps
and set aside for a buffet of
sweets and bowls of traditional
sugar-coated almonds, with
a Renaissance-style sculpted
wedding cake supplying
a spectacular centerpiece.*

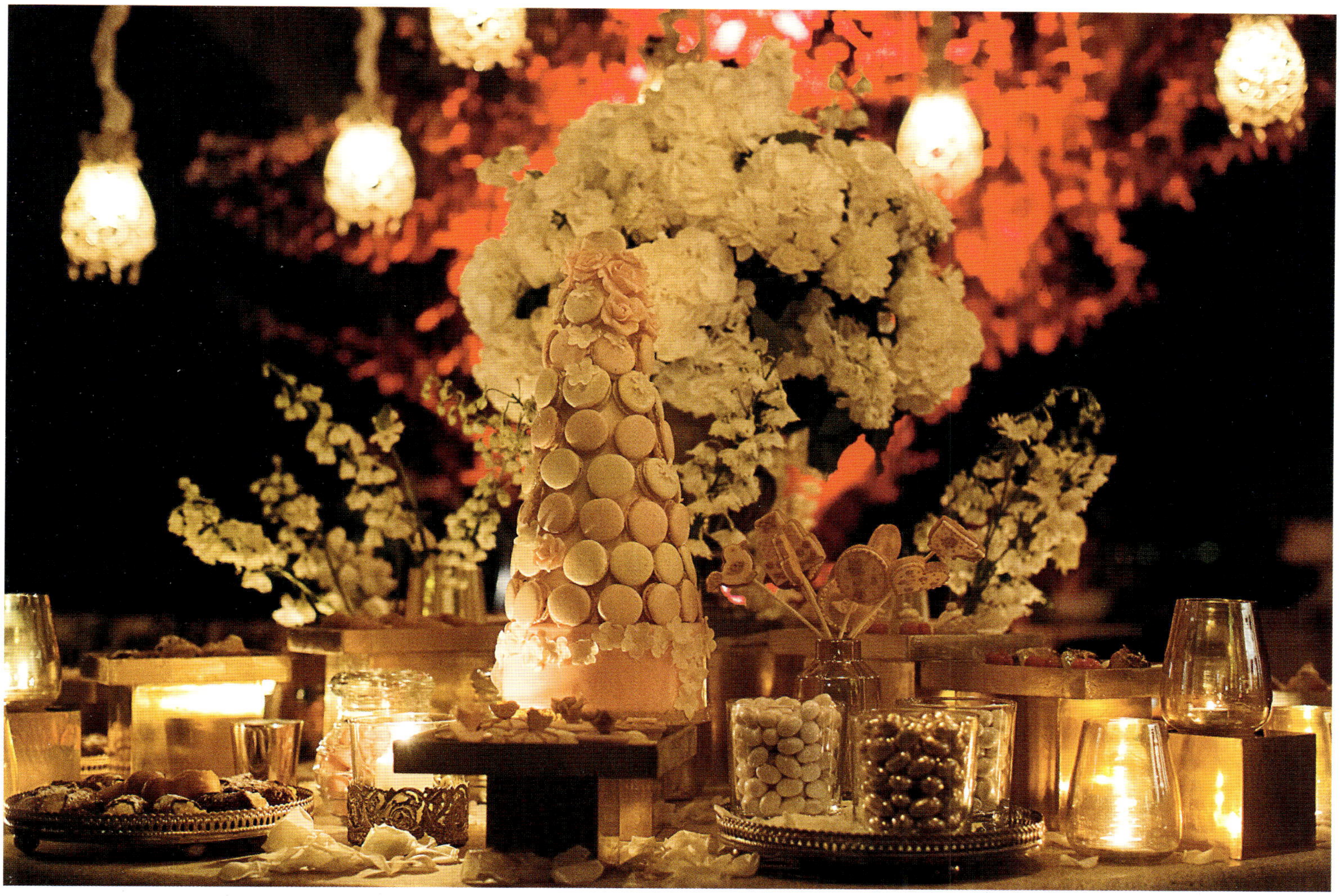

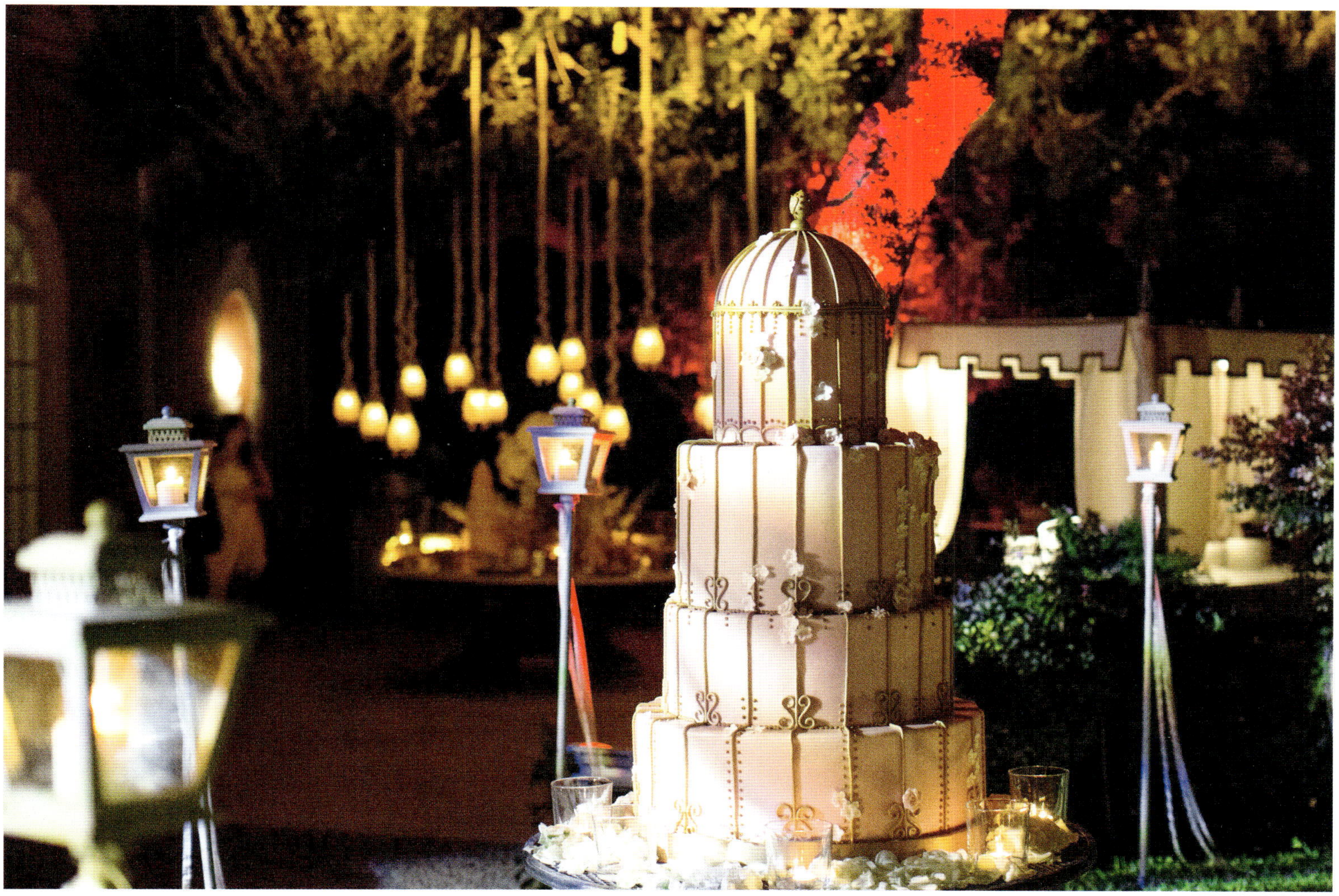

The Magic of Venice

Romantic, magical, timeless. Venice, the city of love *par excellence*, is the setting for a wedding which wends its way from the splendid hotel on the Canal Grande where the bride spent the night before the ceremony to the church of Santa Fosca on the island of Torcello. In Venice organization is key; the launches for the bridal party and the motorboats for the guests all have to be perfectly synchronized.

The bride causes a stir in a ballroom wedding dress with a fairytale skirt in impalpable organza enhanced by two lace trains and a long veil of French Chantilly lace as she enters the Venetian-Byzantine style church, adjacent to the famous basilica of Santa Maria Assunta. The columns of the porch, topped by Byzantine capitals, are decorated in garlands of roses, amaryllis, orchids and spireas. The simple lines of the interior of the church are highlighted by white flower arrangements, in perfect harmony with the sober solemnity of a place of worship.

After the ceremony, the wedding procession makes its way on foot to the nearby Locanda Cipriani for the reception, where pre-dinner drinks are served in the stunning arbors of the garden. The beautiful table settings with their pastel flower arrangements are illuminated by the glow of soft light from Murano blown-glass candelabras, while the menu comprises some of the finest dishes in the Venetian tradition, ending with a mouthwatering buffet of sweetmeats.

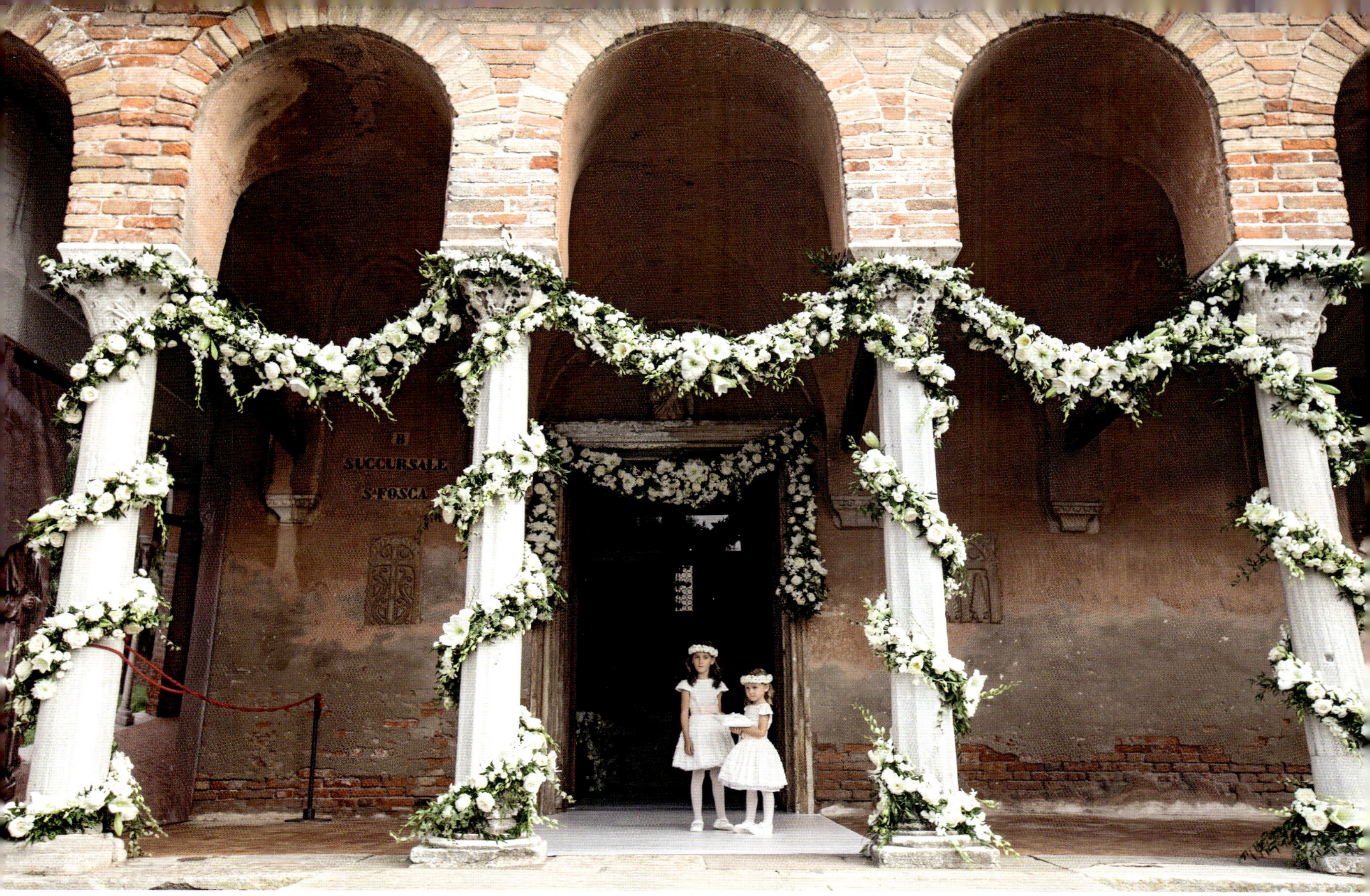
B
SUCCURSALE
S.FOSCA

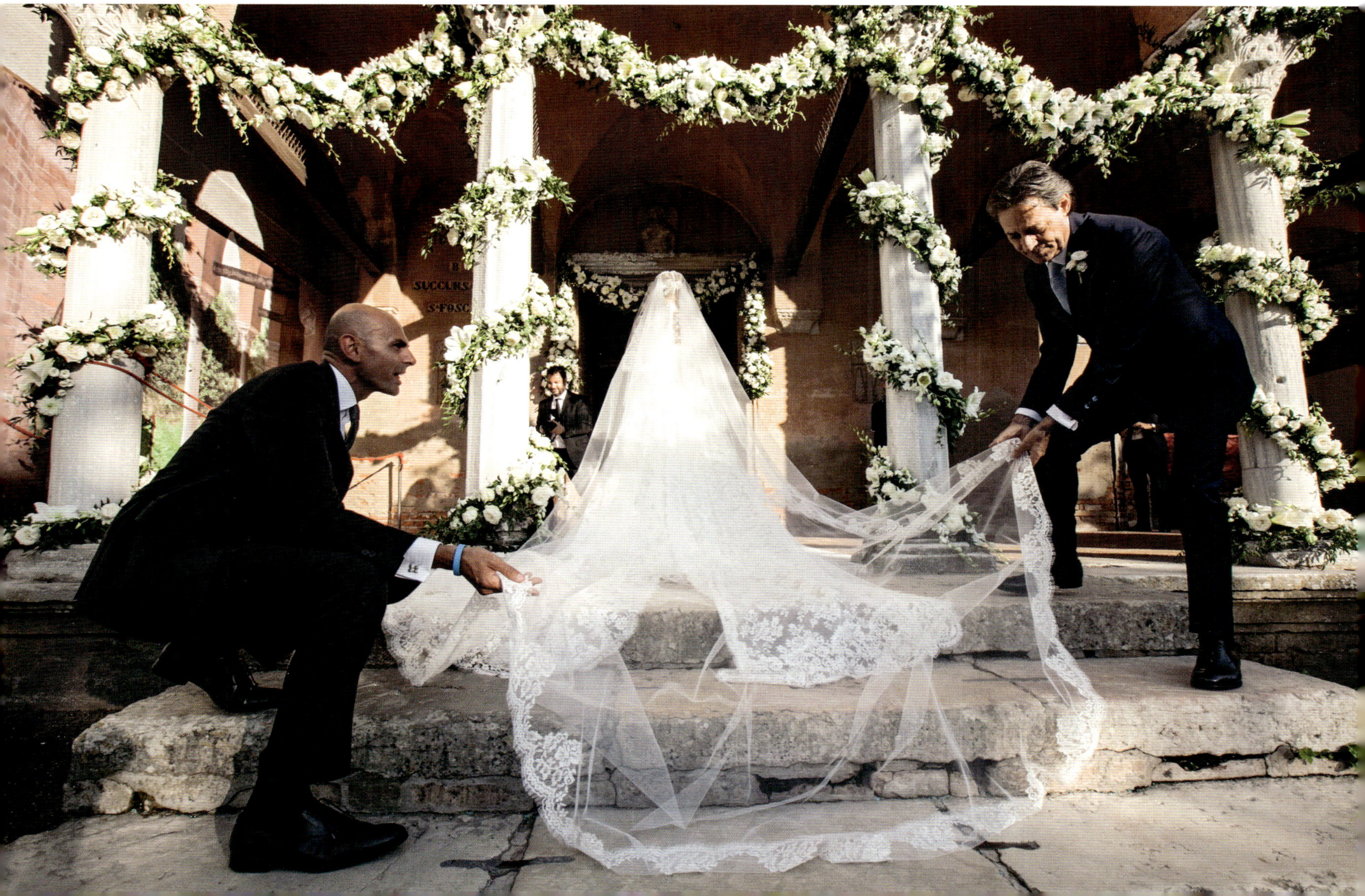

*Garlands of white flowers
lead along the aisle from
the church door to the altar.*

Back to Elegance

The poet Shelley claimed that Lake Como "...*exceeds anything I ever beheld in beauty...*" and undoubtedly one of the most enchanting spots on this most magic of lakes is Cernobbio, with its superb historic villas and palazzos. Here, at the sumptuous Villa d'Este, Gemma and Alberto have chosen to celebrate their September wedding. The church is decorated with delicate touches of powder blue, the perfect background to the traditional white worn by the bride. The dress is an iconic fairytale gown with a huge skirt and Gemma wears a family heirloom of antique lace cleverly crafted onto a long modern veil.

At the reception the bridal couple and their guests enjoy pre-dinner drinks in the scenographic gardens, where comfortable conversation corners have been furnished with sofas and cushions in the event's signature powder blue, with a discreetly aristocratic touch of gold blending in perfectly with such a magnificent setting. The same atmosphere reigns at the long imperial table, where the golden chargers of the settings match the *boules* holding the flower arrangements and, for a final touch of style, the napkins are looped in blue ribbons, echoing the blue in the place cards.

The doors and French windows of the villa have all been wreathed in garlands of leaves and flowers, forming an enchanted gateway to a delicious display of sweets, *petit fours* and bowls of sugared almonds. The cake is impressively decorated *ton sur ton*, presented on a column of boxwood intricately laced with tiny white and peach rosebuds. The velvet darkness of the sky over the lake is suddenly illuminated by a spectacular firework display, a fitting conclusion to a memorable day.

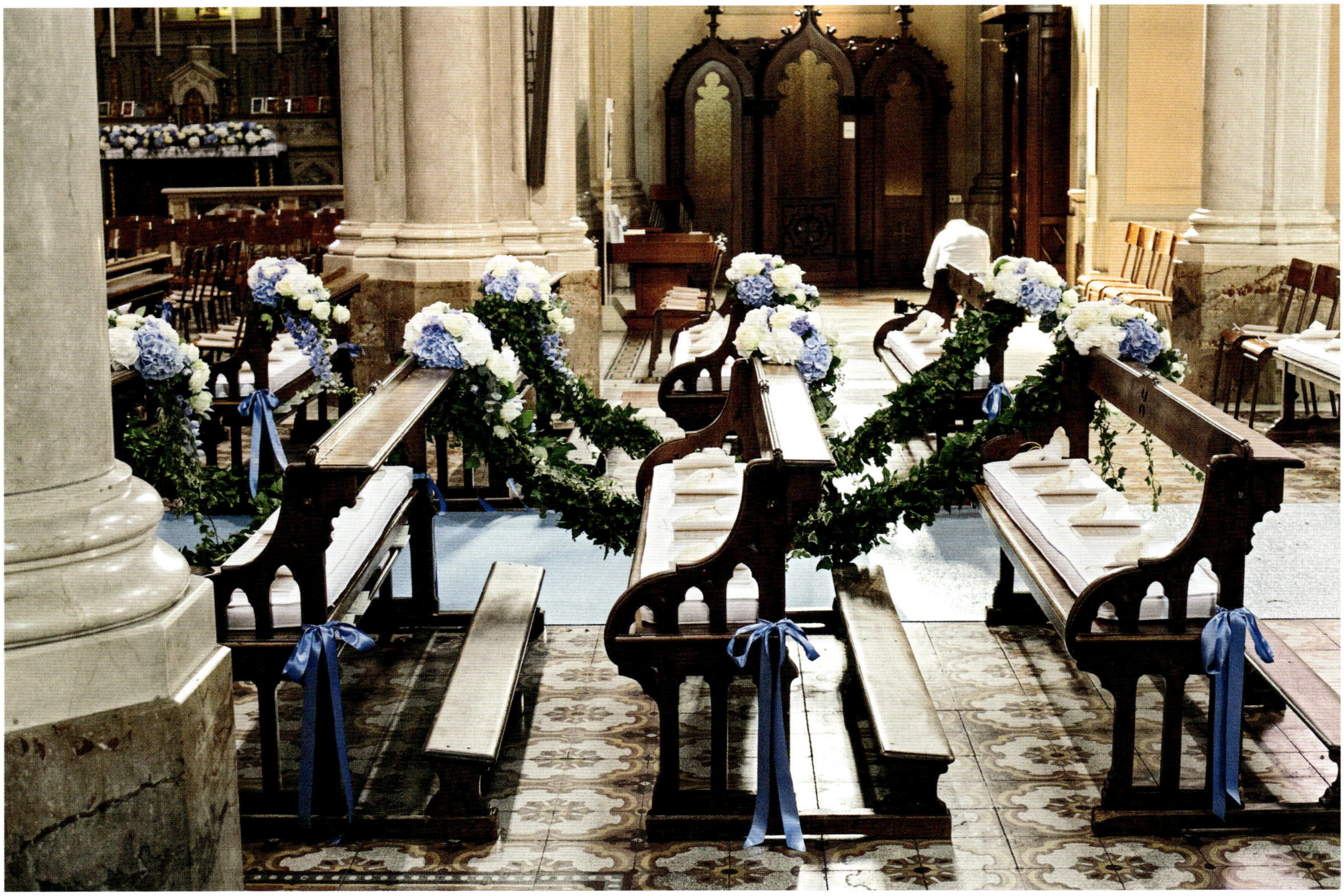

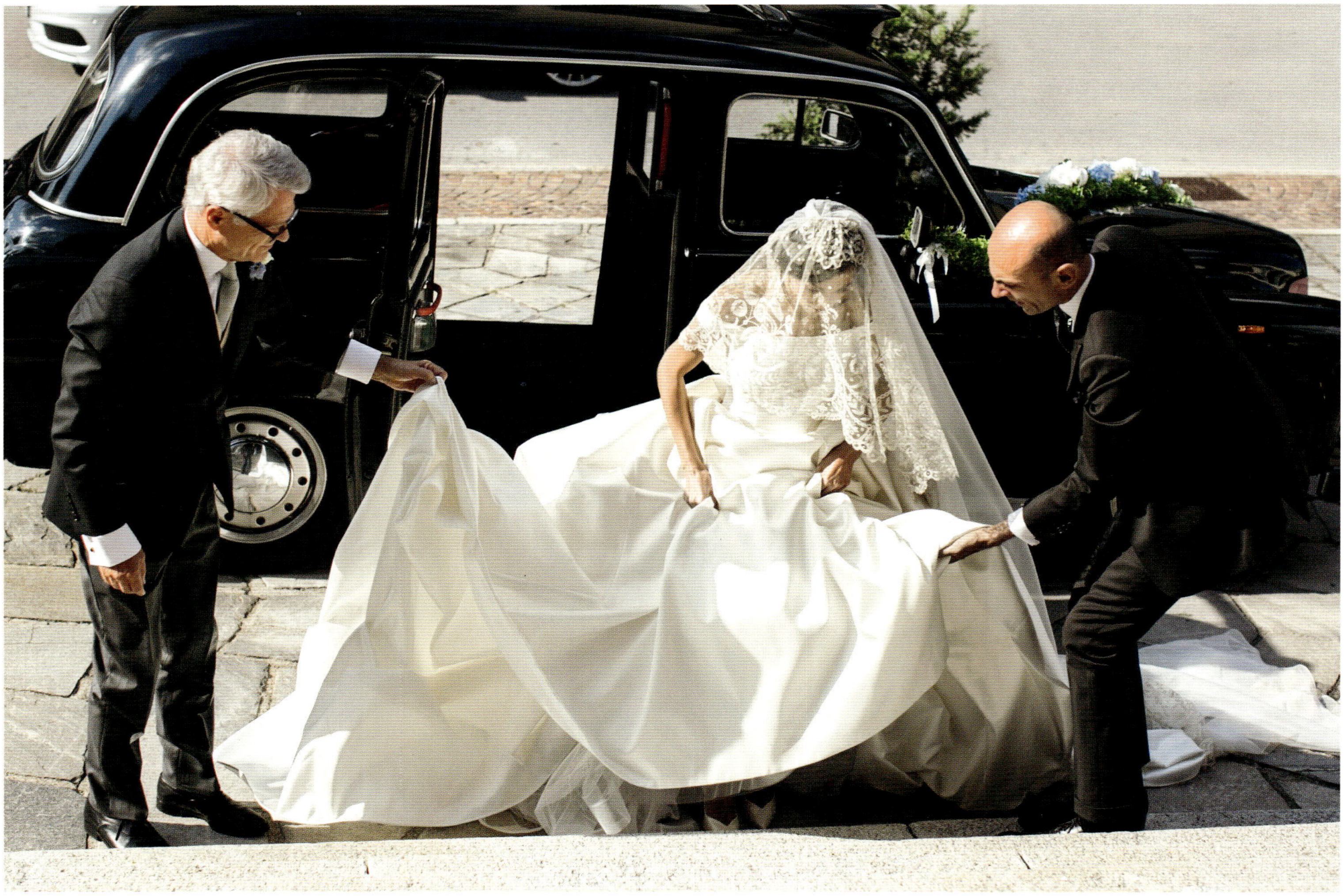

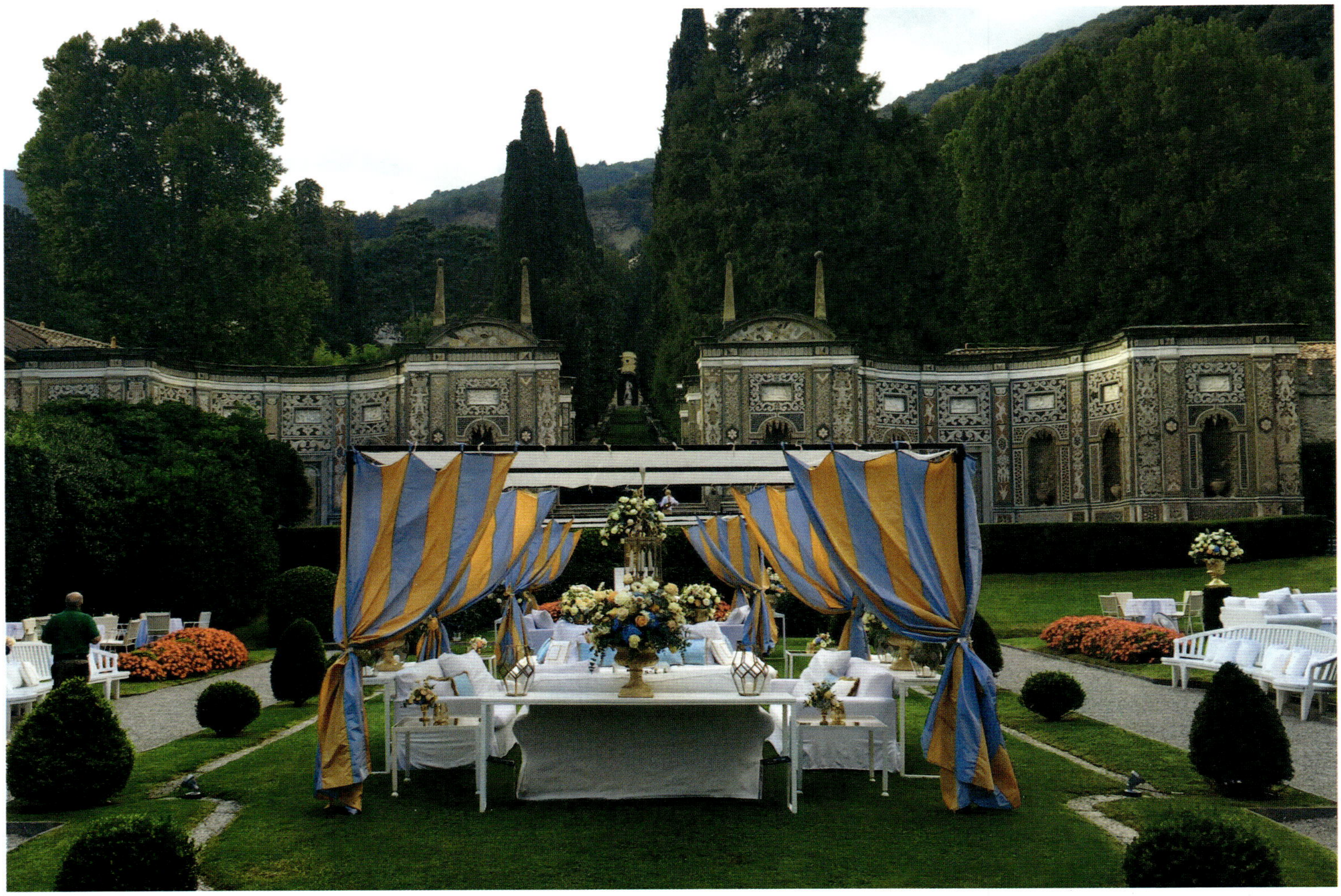

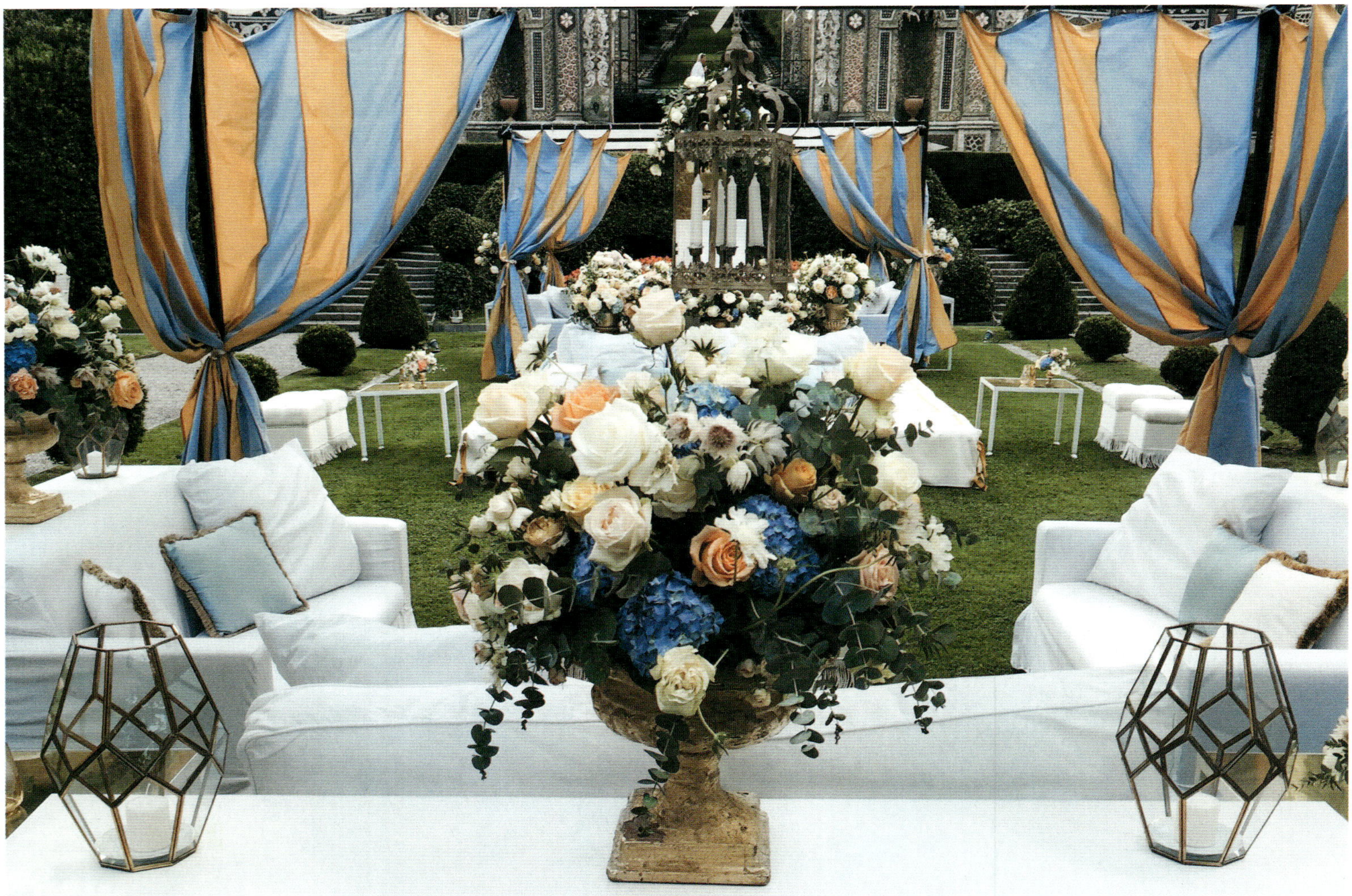

Shades of the Mediterranean Sea

A late summer afternoon on a beach in Salento, in the south of Italy. It is a hot day, so we have prepared turquoise wedding bags for the guests with emergency supplies comprising a bottle of water, the rice traditionally thrown at Italian weddings in place of confetti and paper handkerchiefs to mop up those "tears of joy".

The ceremony takes place at an altar erected against the sea under a bower of four arches wreathed in the elegant simplicity of baby's breath entwined with white roses and accessed along a path strewn with rose petals.

The reception takes place in a marvelous *masseria*, one of the country houses the Puglia region is famous for, its lawns dotted with comfortable sofas and turquoise and white striped cushions, evocative of the exquisite turquoise blue of the Mediterranean Sea. White dominates in the candelabras and flower arrangements.

Evening has fallen and the long tables prepared for the dinner are decorated with branches of white coral in homage to the stunning seabed off the coast of Salento, while swathes of white organza illuminated by blue spotlights recreate a romantic marine environment.

*A turquoise fishing boat
does duty as an unusual cake
stand, while the wedding
favors, simple boxes tied up in
turquoise and white ribbon,
are arranged on a charmingly
traditional street vendor's cart.*

A Romantic Palazzo

A Palladian villa along the Brenta Riviera provides the perfect venue for a romantic wedding reminiscent of times gone by. The perfectly-executed calligraphy of the hand-written wedding invitations set the mood for the occasion, which culminates in a banquet under the *trompe l'oeil* frescoes decorating the magnificent ballroom, painted almost four centuries ago in 1652. This wonderful palazzo was once the residence of one of the last Doges of Venice, and the style of the reception is a homage to so much history.

The prevailing atmosphere is decidedly romantic, and this is reflected in the bride's sumptuous dress, embellished with crystals, and in the delicate diamante comb in her hair. A horse-drawn carriage takes the bridal couple from the church in the historical centre of Padua to their reception in the palazzo, providing an original backdrop to some of the wedding photographs.

For the banquet in the ballroom guests are seated at long imperial tables under huge candelabras filled with scented roses, the leitmotiv flower for the whole wedding, while original butterfly-ballerinas provide the entertainment amidst an exciting display of lights during the cutting of the cake.

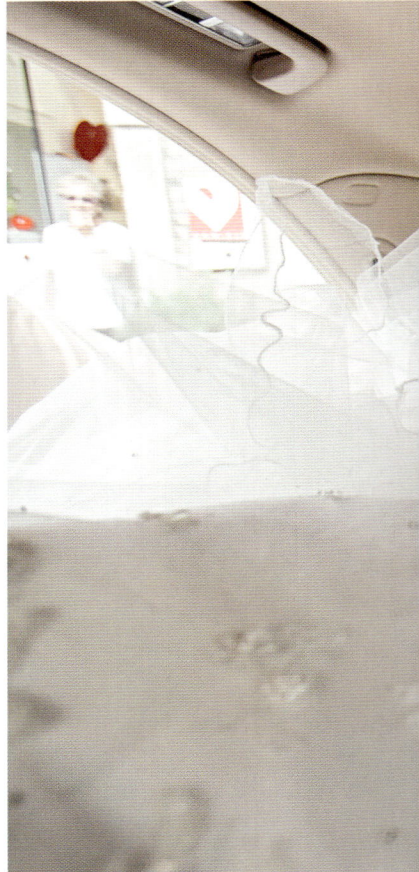

The Romanesque-Gothic church of San Nicolò in Padua, with 15th-century frescoes, is decorated with round bouquets of white roses set at just above head height at the end of the pews all along the aisle, a theme reprised outside the church.

*Conversation corners in the
portico of the palazzo under
a cascade of dozens of different
antique chandeliers, complete
with elegant white sofas,
lanterns and a profusion
of hints of gold, with matching
decorations for the delicious
buffet of sweetmeats.*

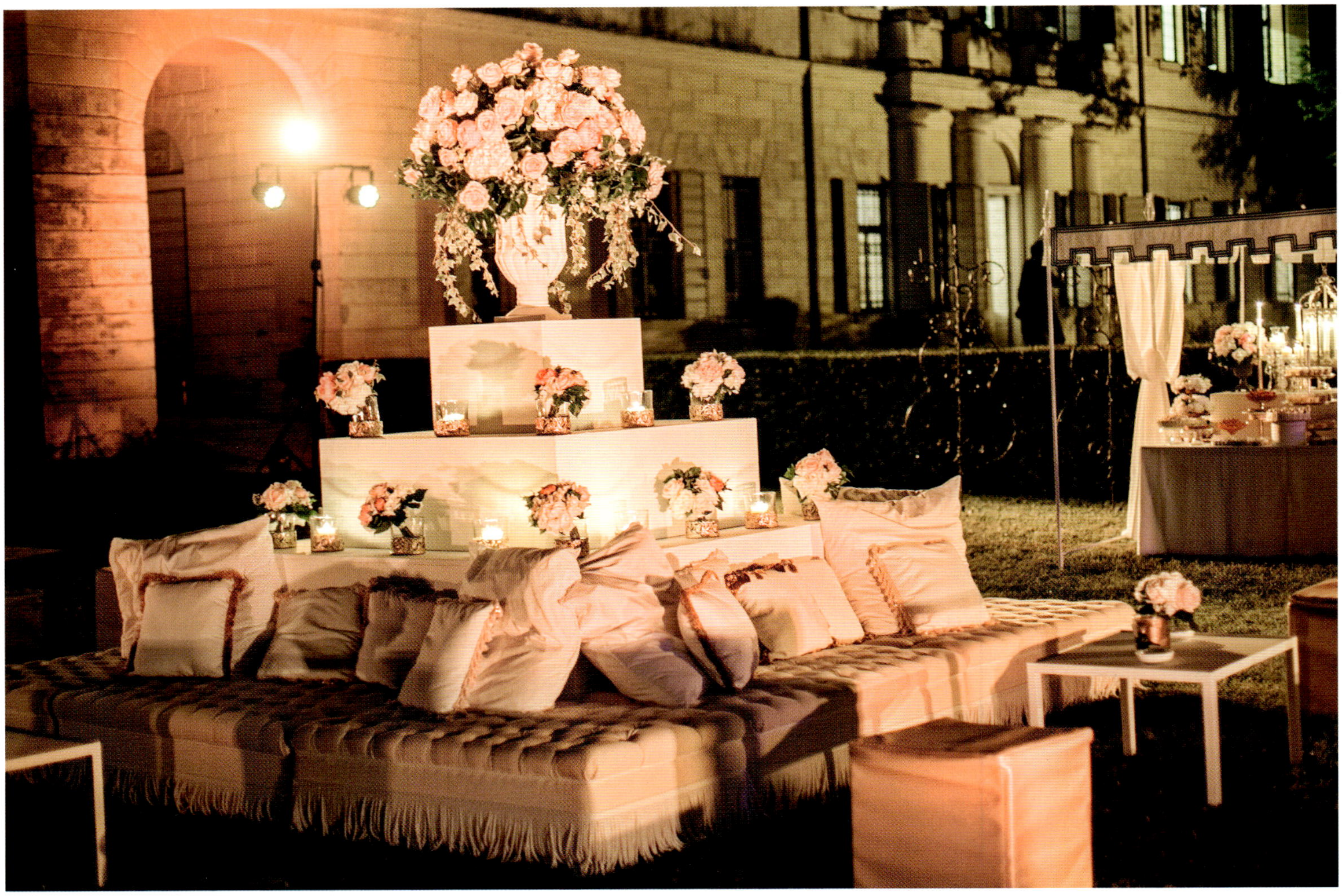

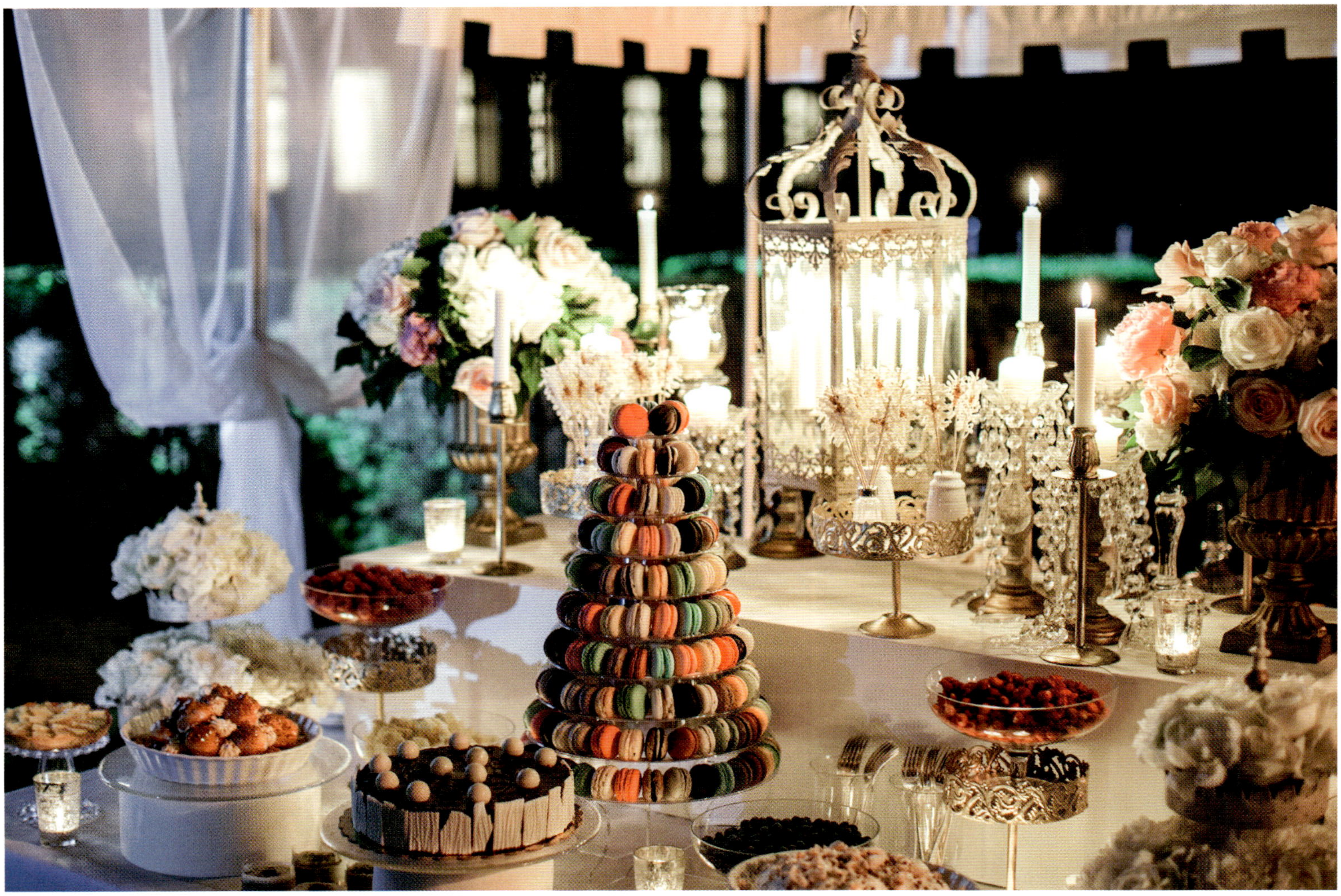

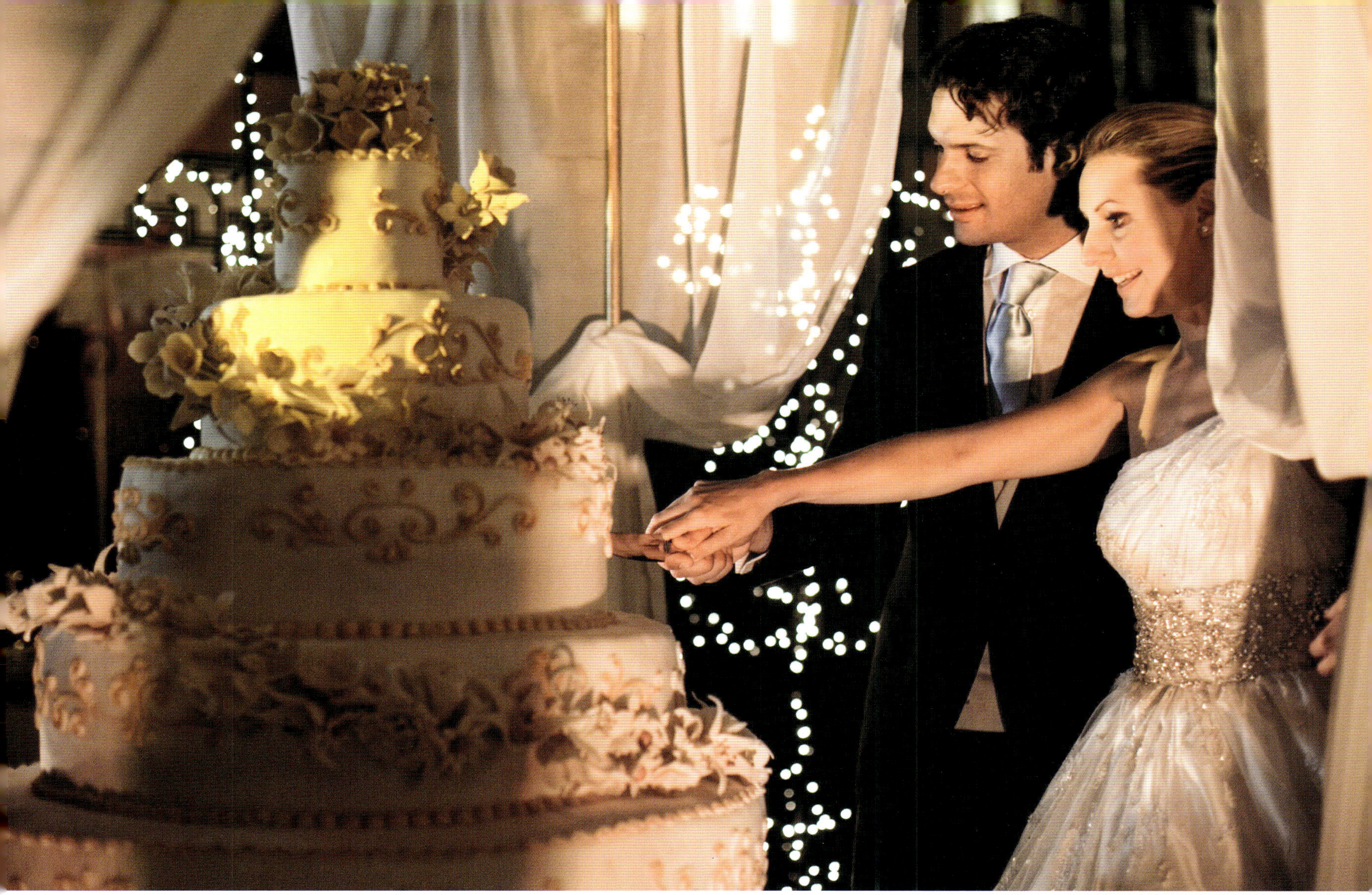

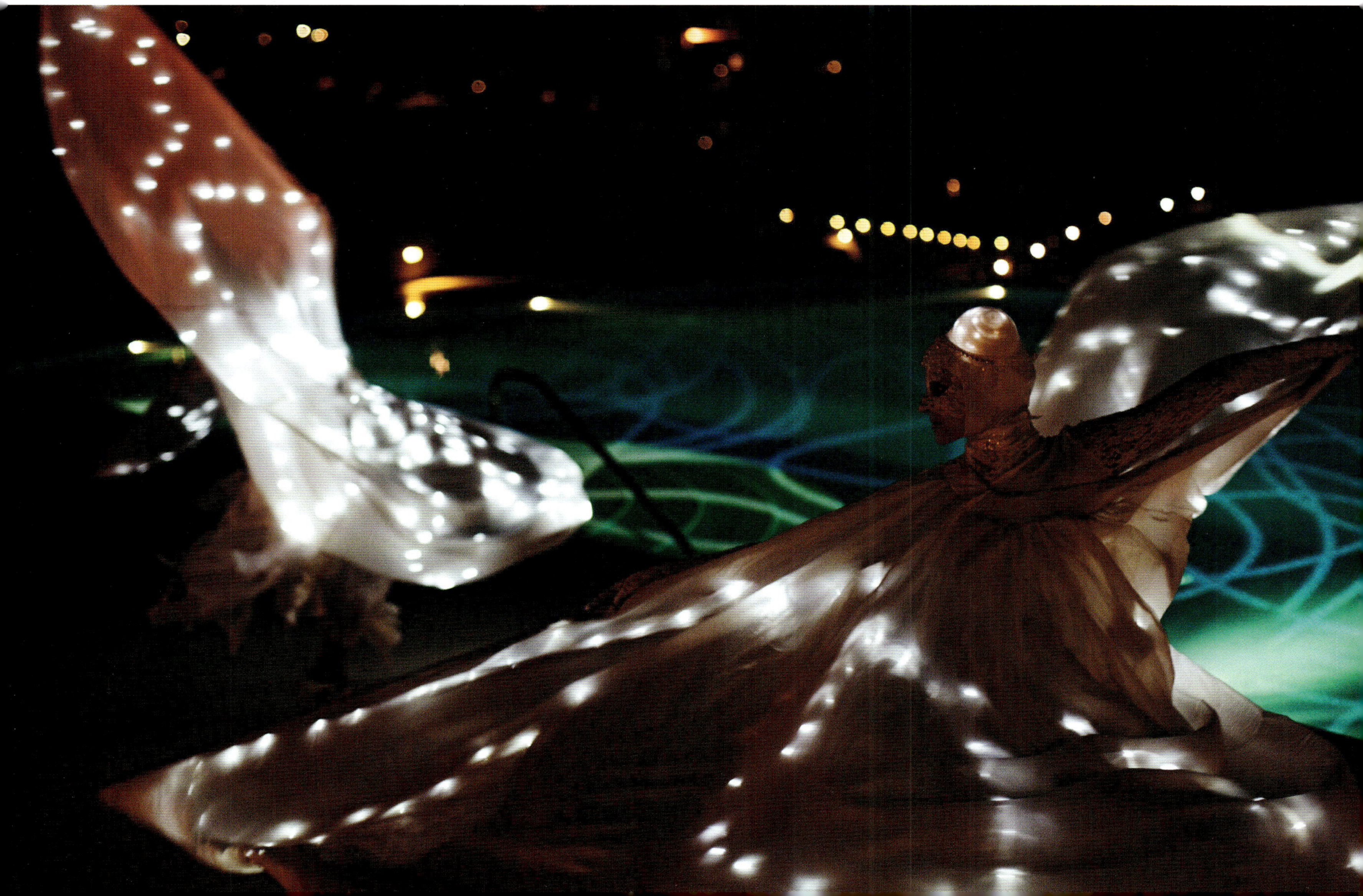

Country Chic

A wedding on a country estate in Tuscany. Rustic elegance is the keynote here, reflected in the wheat sheaves entwined with ivy and olive branches used to decorate the cathedral of Chiusi and the semi arches of boxwood hung with wreaths of wheat which line the aisle. Set before the altar is an antique French *prie-dieu* in pale green pickled wood with ivory-colored cushions and poufs for the bride and groom.

To emphasize the simplicity of the whole occasion the aperitif is staged in the vineyard, with gazebos in white organza over white sofas and rustic tables of rough pallets set on bales of straw and decorated with white flower arrangements in olivewood bowls and ears of wheat. Another conversation piece are the unusual installations: "stalls" of herbs and local produce dotted around the estate.

The convivial atmosphere of informality continues when the 200 guests sit down to eat at two long tables on a wooden dais under a linen awning. The tables are set simply, but with great care: candlelight, unbleached linen napkins bordered in white, hand thrown local terracotta chargers made from the red clay the area is famous for and wood and cork bowls for the flower arrangements. The buffet of sweetmeats is set out in a rustic dresser filled with homemade biscuits and jam tarts, confirming the country theme. The wedding cake is designed in stacked imitation wicker baskets of cleverly woven icing and decorated with sugar garlands framing mini portions of cake.

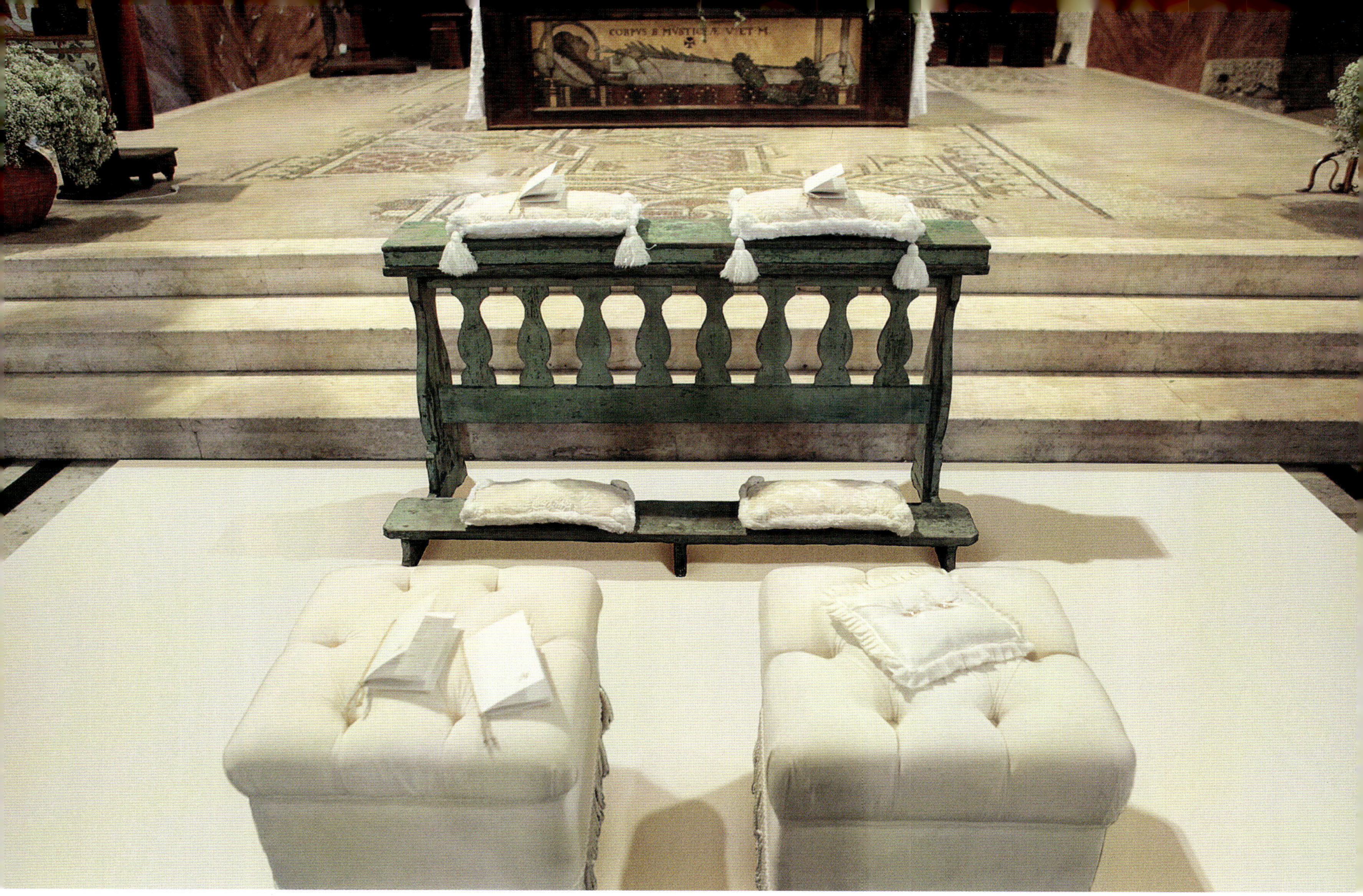

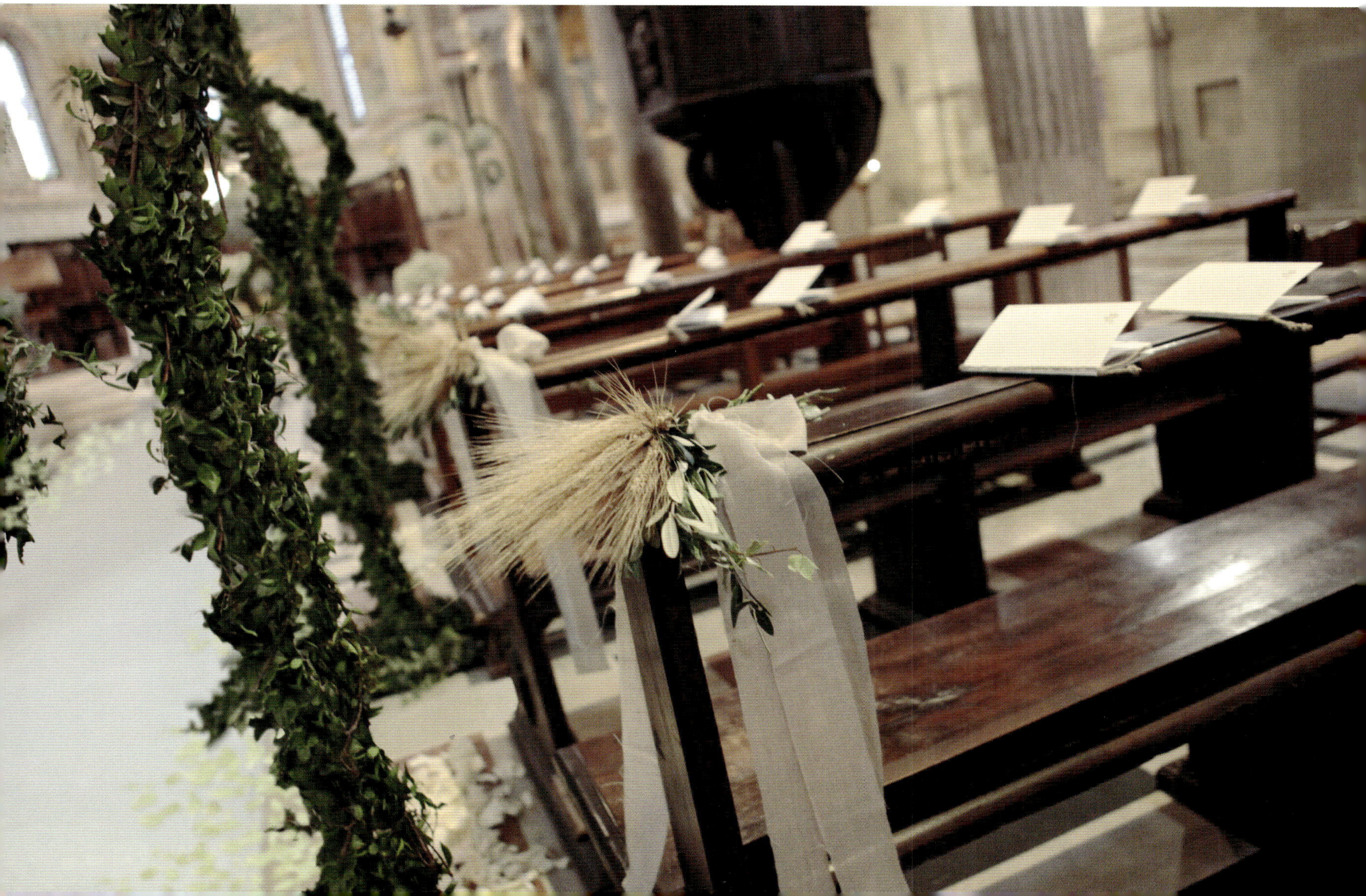

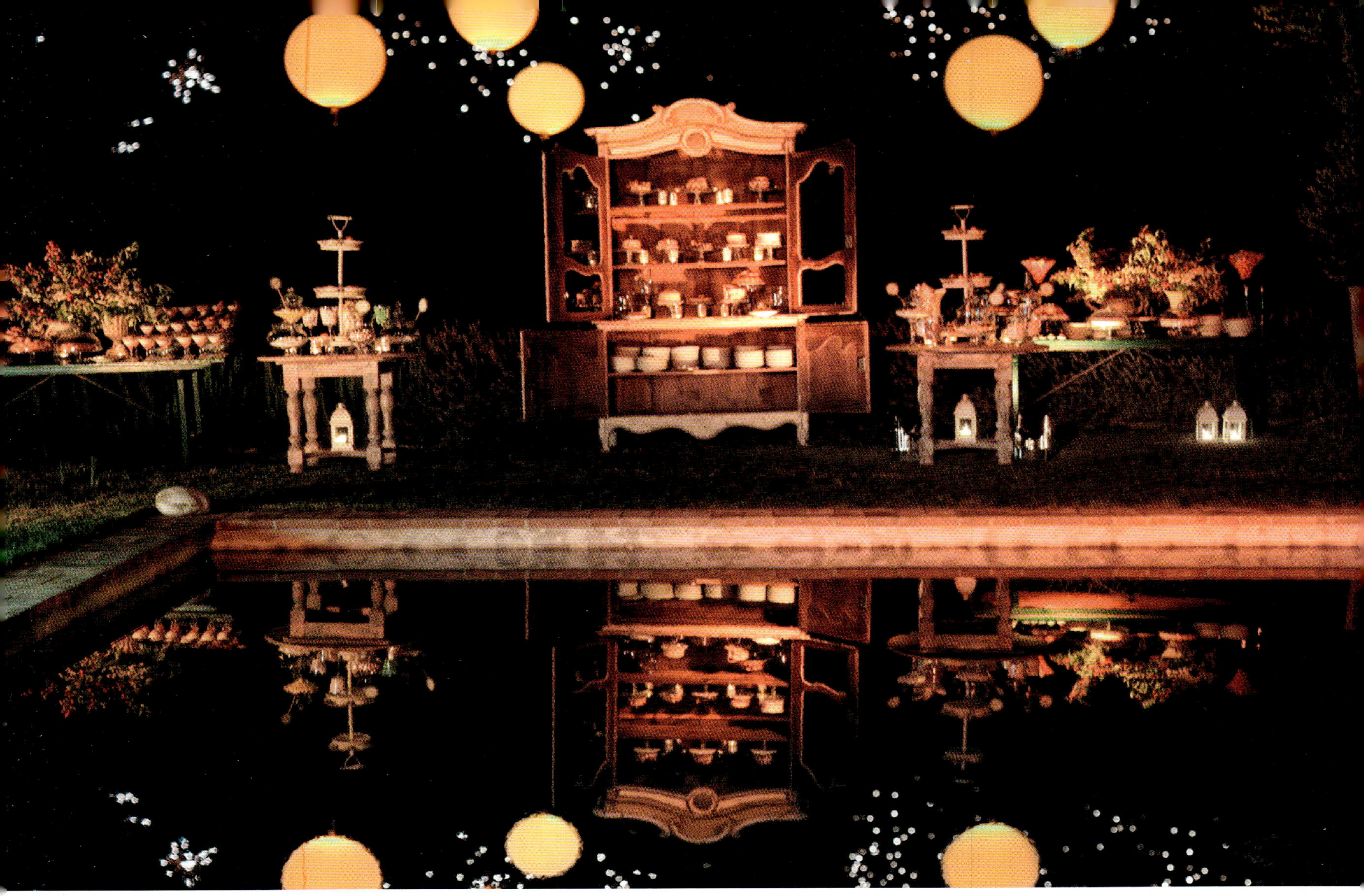

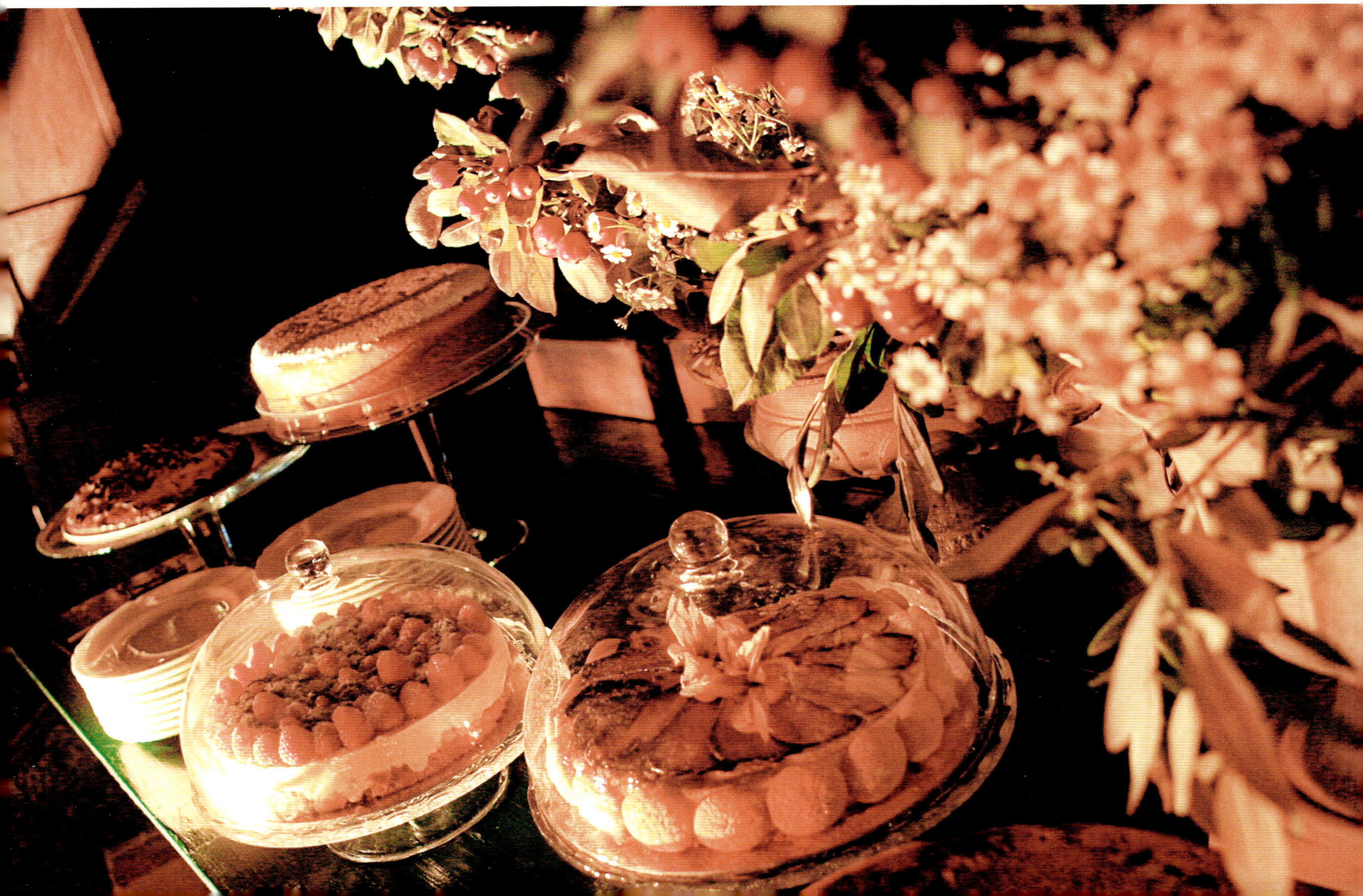

Symphony in White

The Basilica of Santa Maria in Aracoeli, on the summit of the smallest of Rome's seven hills, is famous for its dramatic sweep of steps standing side by side with the courtyard designed by Michelangelo for Rome's Renaissance town hall. This is one of Rome's artistic treasures, a spectacular setting for truly splendid weddings. Gold abounds, starting with the gold leaf on the moldings of the sixteenth-century coffered ceiling. How to avoid clashing with this sumptuous interior? The best solution proves to be total white, with rows of white urns on simple square columns filled with white roses and orchids.

The pews have been draped in swathes of white cloth in keeping with Roman tradition and paired with antique gilt chairs with matching white seats. On each seat a mini wedding bag full of rice to shower the bridal couple with as they emerge from the church. A splendid stage for a splendid bride! Preceded by adorable little flower girls scattering petals, she wears a white mermaid lace dress with a veil seven meters long, emphasizing her tall, slim figure. Total enchantment.

*White also predominates
at the reception that evening
on the Via Appia Antica.
The dress code specified
that guests should wear a
touch of gold, echoing the gold
in the taffeta runners
on the tables, on the place
cards and on the gilded
organza napkin ribbons.*

The Enchanted Wood

Anna and Philip are from London, but have chosen a marvelous country house in a Tuscan village for their June wedding. The bride wants a simple ceremony surrounded by nature, so we have set a romantic stage in a charming dell in the woods. The splendid bride and groom wend their way through the trees to the soft sound of violins and a harp on the notes of a string quartet, as the branches appear to bow down in a tender gesture of greeting to their guests.

Amidst the leafy green a delicate bower decked with garlands of flowers and hung with organza awaits them. The bride and groom pledge their troth blessed by the sun, making its appearance on this midsummer's day after a morning storm. The bride wears a dress with a lace bodice and a soft, A-line skirt gathered at the waist by a broad sash of pale pink silk tied in a bow. Her shoes are equally lovely, but essentially comfortable – allowing her to walk gracefully and naturally!

*The bouquet is very unusual
and Anna falls in love with
it at first sight. It comprises
proteas, typical flowers
of the southern hemisphere
common in South Africa
– a homage to the origins of
the bridegroom – together
with peonies, sweet peas,
roses and mock orange, tied
together with a silver organza
ribbon. We keep it fresh in the
vintage bathtub of the bride's
suite, where she can admire it
right up until the last minute
before the ceremony.*

Country chic: the pre-dinner finger food buffet is laid out on glass tables supported by wine casks, while the conversation corners comprise comfortable wrought-iron chairs and sofas and bleached wood coffee tables. Very Tuscany.

A Castle in Winter

What better place to celebrate that special day during the chill of winter than in the warmth of a fairytale castle? Chiara and Fabio have chosen Rivalta Castle on the hills above Piacenza for their reception. A Saturday in December, Christmas is in the air: the castle's frescoed ballroom, over a thousand years old, is warmed by a blazing fire in the huge hearth and the colorful flower arrangements and decorations.

The table is a riot of reds, purples, lilacs and shades of mauve to match the bright silk of the place mats and everything is ready to receive the guests after drinks in the atmospheric castle wine cellar, which has been decorated with flowers in hanging wooden tubs in the signature colors of this wedding. After dinner the bride and groom cut the cake by the light of the stars in the courtyard (glassed over for the occasion to protect guests from the cold) under the romantic walls of the castle.

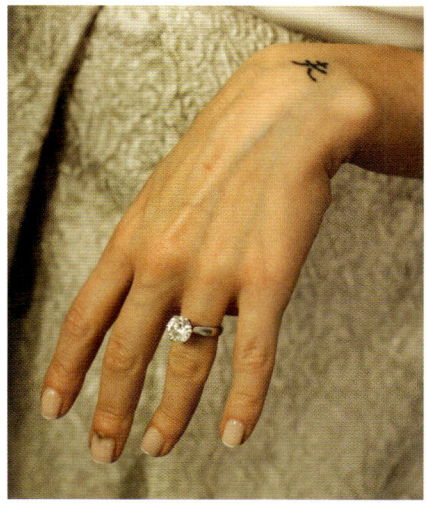

December: the entrance
to the little parish church
of San Martino in the village
of Rivalta is lined with
snow-covered miniature
Christmas trees. Inside
a succession of heart-shaped
leafy arches entwined with
white flowers line the aisle
to wish the newlyweds luck.

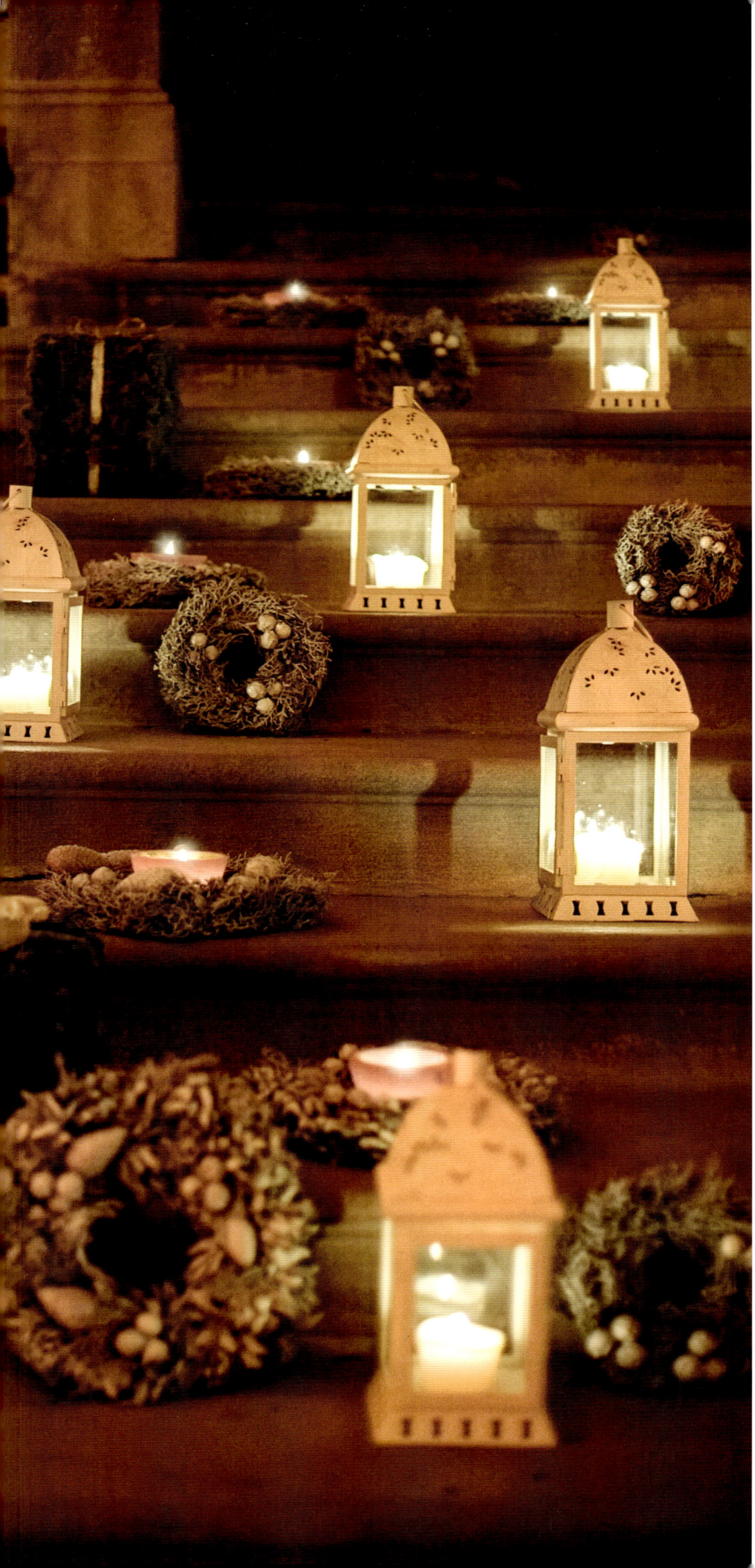
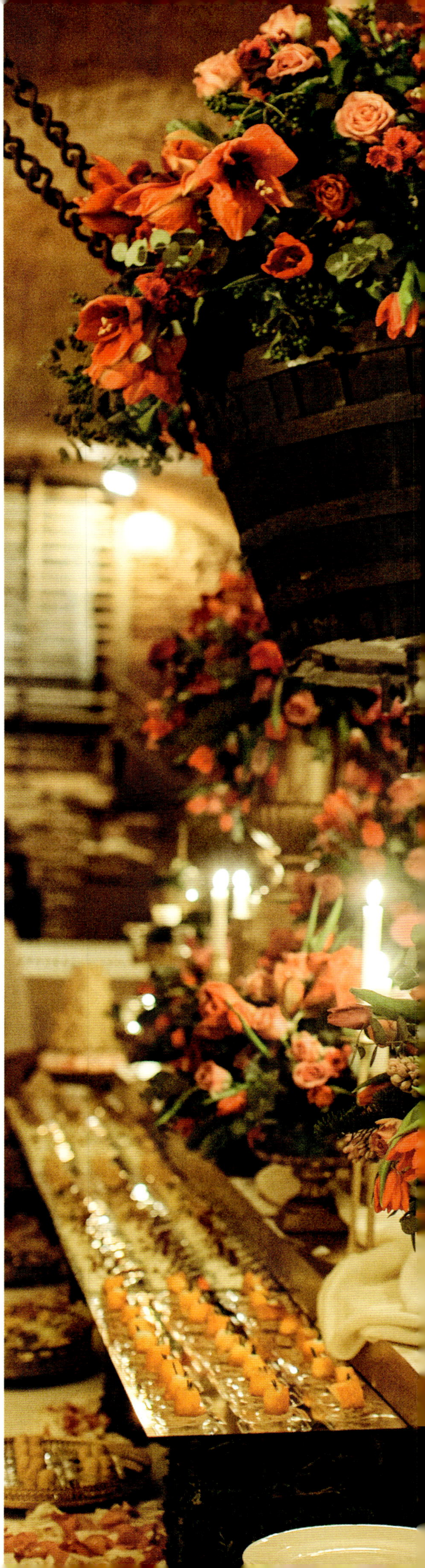

The napkins are
monogrammed with
an embroidered
pomegranate. The white,
red and gold color scheme
of the table settings
is carefully orchestrated
down to the last detail of
the place cards. Dancers
in 19th-century costume
entertain the guests with
waltzes during dinner.

Village Rites

Chiara and Robin have chosen a medieval hamlet in the province of Siena in beautiful Tuscany for a wedding where rustic charm meets modern design. An original weekend with a wealth of friends from all four corners of the globe, many of them involved in the fashion world like the bride and groom. The three-day celebration starts with a dinner on Friday, followed by the wedding on Saturday and a Sunday brunch in the courtyard. At the heart of the village is a little piazza, surrounded by medieval houses, with the tiny church where Chiara and Robin are to be married. The church is so small we have had to set rows of chairs, each with its obligatory wedding bag, for some of the guests outside in the piazza!

The bride has chosen glamour as the key mood for the sophisticated *mise en place*, with designer flower arrangements in a delicate palette of six colors ranging from white to ivory, champagne, powder pink and misty rose, with a touch of gold for warmth. The bridesmaids wear the palest powder pink in different dress styles.

After dinner, before cutting the cake which is surrounded by a riot of roses, the courtyard is transformed by a stunning light designer display accompanied by the breathtaking acrobatics of the *Cirque du Soleil* performers, the event's special guests.

White awnings with just
a hint of color define
conversation corners with
white sofas under the starry
sky in the ample cloister of the
village monastery, echoed
by seating arrangements in
the courtyard and next to
the swimming pool where the
formal dining tables are set.

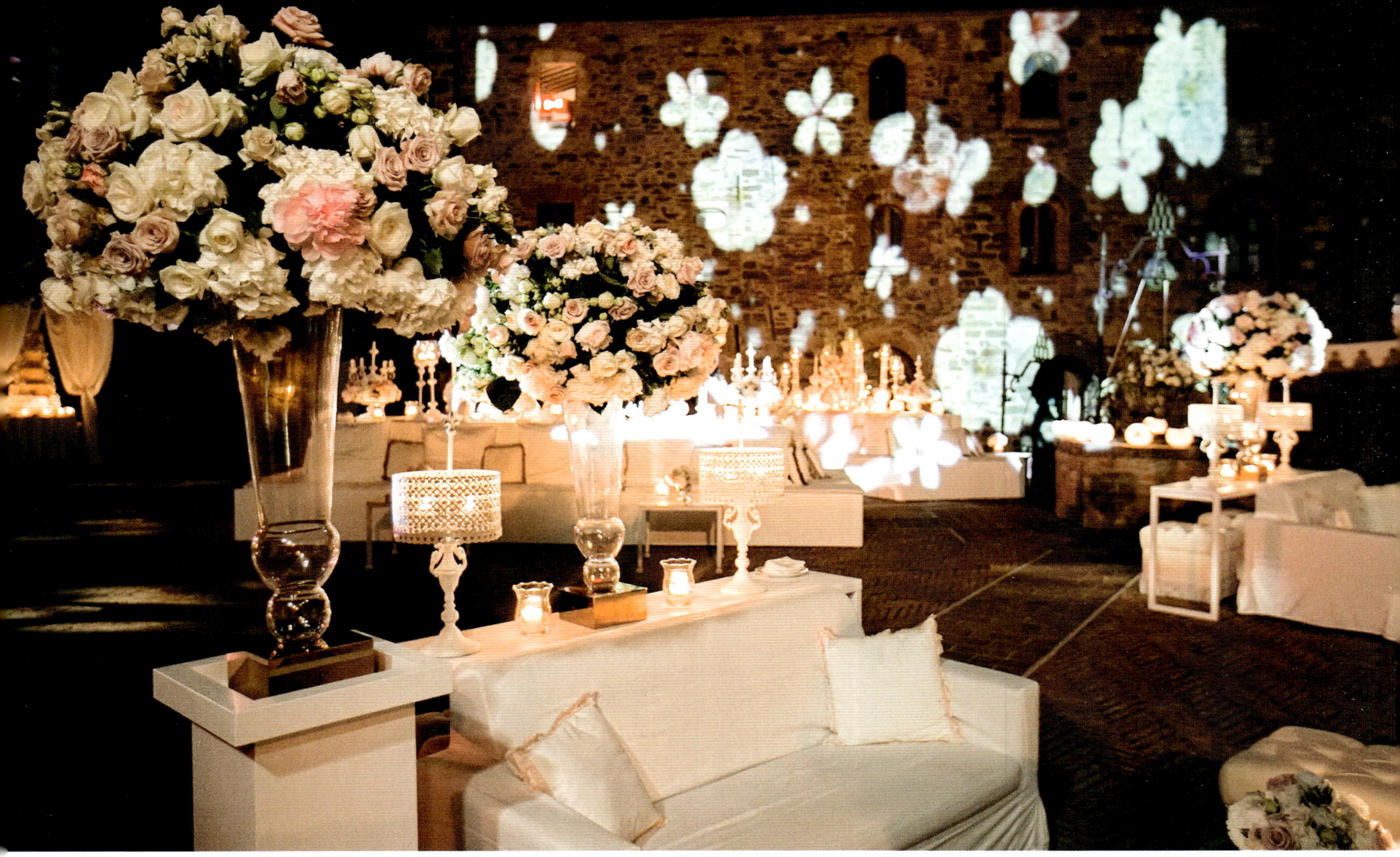

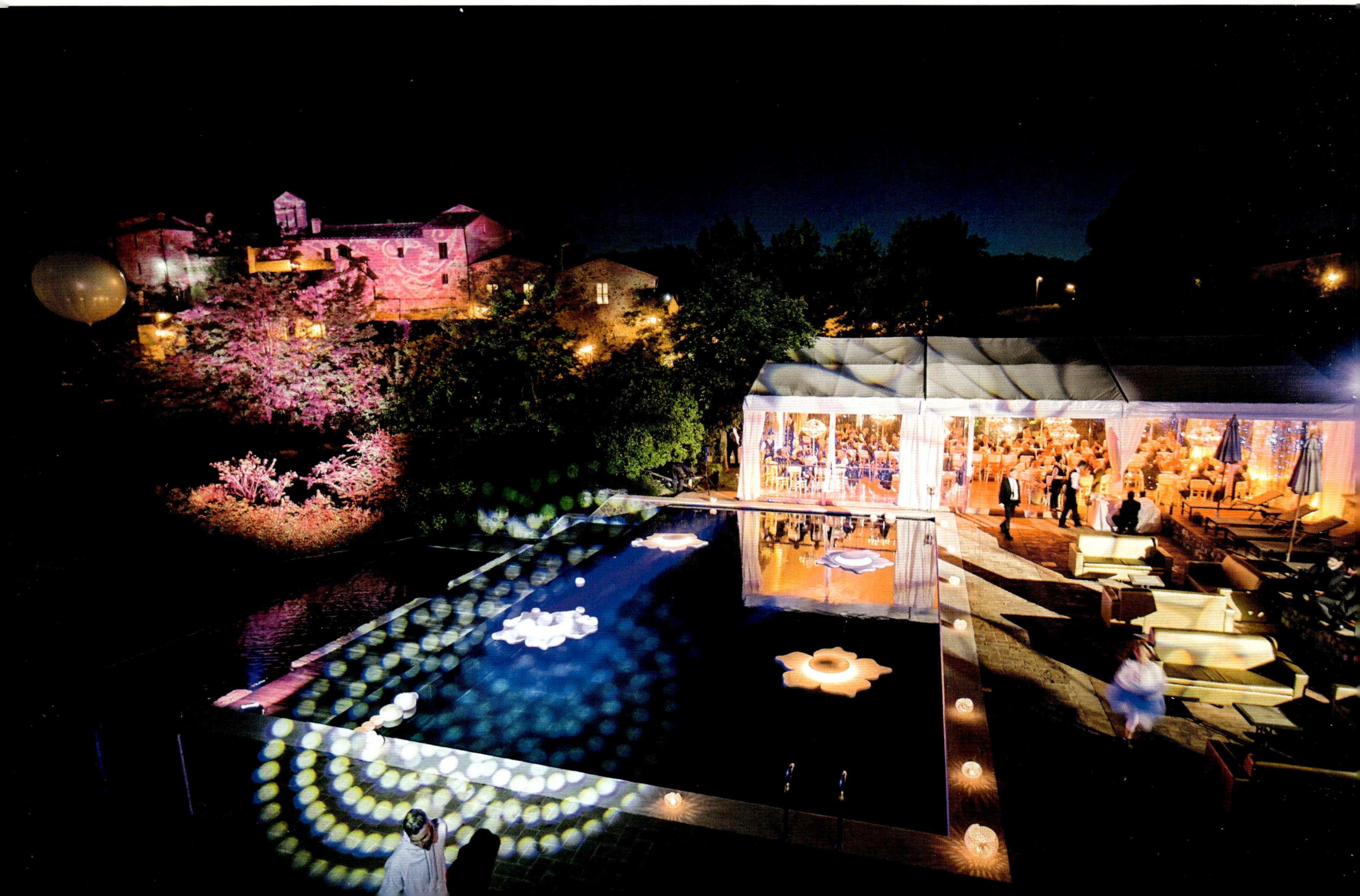

The Magic of the Amalfi Coast

Ravello is where the deep blue of the Mediterranean Sea touches the intense blue of the Mediterranean sky, a dream-like setting; "a promise of happiness", as Stendhal wrote. The perfect place to celebrate a very special wedding. Everything is ready for the occasion: the cathedral has been decked with trees, transforming it into a sort of leafy bower. The green branches arch over the aisle to welcome the bride, radiant in her one shoulder dress, its bodice embroidered with semiprecious stones. The ample skirt is in feather-light floating chiffon and she wears a sheer organza veil over the whole ensemble. The bouquet, always a focal point carefully designed to match the bride's dress and personal tastes, has been a symbol of marriage since classical times and is traditionally offered to the gods to invoke protection and fertility. Here it is declined in all the simple, timeless beauty of lily-of-the-valley with a garland of English roses.

After the ceremony the guests walk to the Hotel Caruso for the reception. Close family are seated at an imperial table in a dining room carpeted in grass, deliberately designed to emphasize continuity with the splendid gardens outside. The *mise en place* comprises a service of traditional white local tableware made especially for this occasion, but the total white effect is cleverly set off by the powder green of prickly pears, eucalyptus leaves, tall stems of amaryllis and orchids.

The hotel gardens and terraces, boasting a simply breathtaking view over the Amalfi coast, host a village fiesta for the occasion, with barbecues and "stalls" dispensing a mouthwatering array of local delicacies. The protagonist is the light design project, with the garden wrapped in a son et lumière *architecture enhancing the impression of village festivities. Music and dancing are the prelude to the cutting of the cake.*

Local specialties of cannoli, babà, patisserie flavored with Amalfi lemons, petit fours and the traditional sugared almonds surround the splendid wedding cake, actually a supporting structure for carefully arranged single portions.

Invitation to the Grand Hotel

In the centre of Milan, just a stone's throw from the famous Duomo, the church of Sant'Alessandro was founded by Cardinal Federico Borromeo, who appropriately makes an appearance in Manzoni's famous novel *The Betrothed*. It is the start of winter and a chill, but sunny, day awaits our bride, wrapped in an endless veil with edges embroidered in simple whorls. She processes down an aisle transformed into an *allée* of silver birch trees hung with garlands of baby's breath and white flowers supporting a thousand candles, a uniquely warm touch of glowing light turning the Baroque interior of the church into a fairytale wonderland.

Sober elegance, in keeping with Milan's renowned tradition of understatement, is the keynote at the reception held at the Grand Hotel, a venue which transforms any event into a great occasion. In the dining room the long imperial head table is surrounded by smaller round tables, all decorated with bouquets of white flowers wreathed in baby's breath.

The wedding cake is another homage to winter, with icing stars and snowflakes and clear sugar crystals which echo the huge chandeliers lighting the scene.

The seating plan is
amusingly presented
as a board of tasseled
room keys, in keeping
with the venue.

Sunset over the Sea

A hotel terrace poised above the Mediterranean Sea opposite the enchanted isle of Capri. A romantic sunset rendered magical by a solo voice *a cappella*, hymning the special blessing celebrating Alessandro and Yanel's union. Friends and family are visibly moved as they gather round the happy couple. The decorative theme chosen for this very special day is a decidedly masculine nautical look in tones of blue and white.

After the blessing against the backdrop of the sea at sunset (and what scenario could be more moving?), on a warm day in September, it is time for the guests to move on to the sailor-themed party with flags and lanterns, white sofas with white and blue cushions dotted around the terraces, tables decorated with boats and sailing ships and a menu dominated by fish and seafood. And to set sail together over the great sea of life, a fleet of tiny boats with portions of the wedding cake, their sails embroidered with the monogram of the couple in blue.

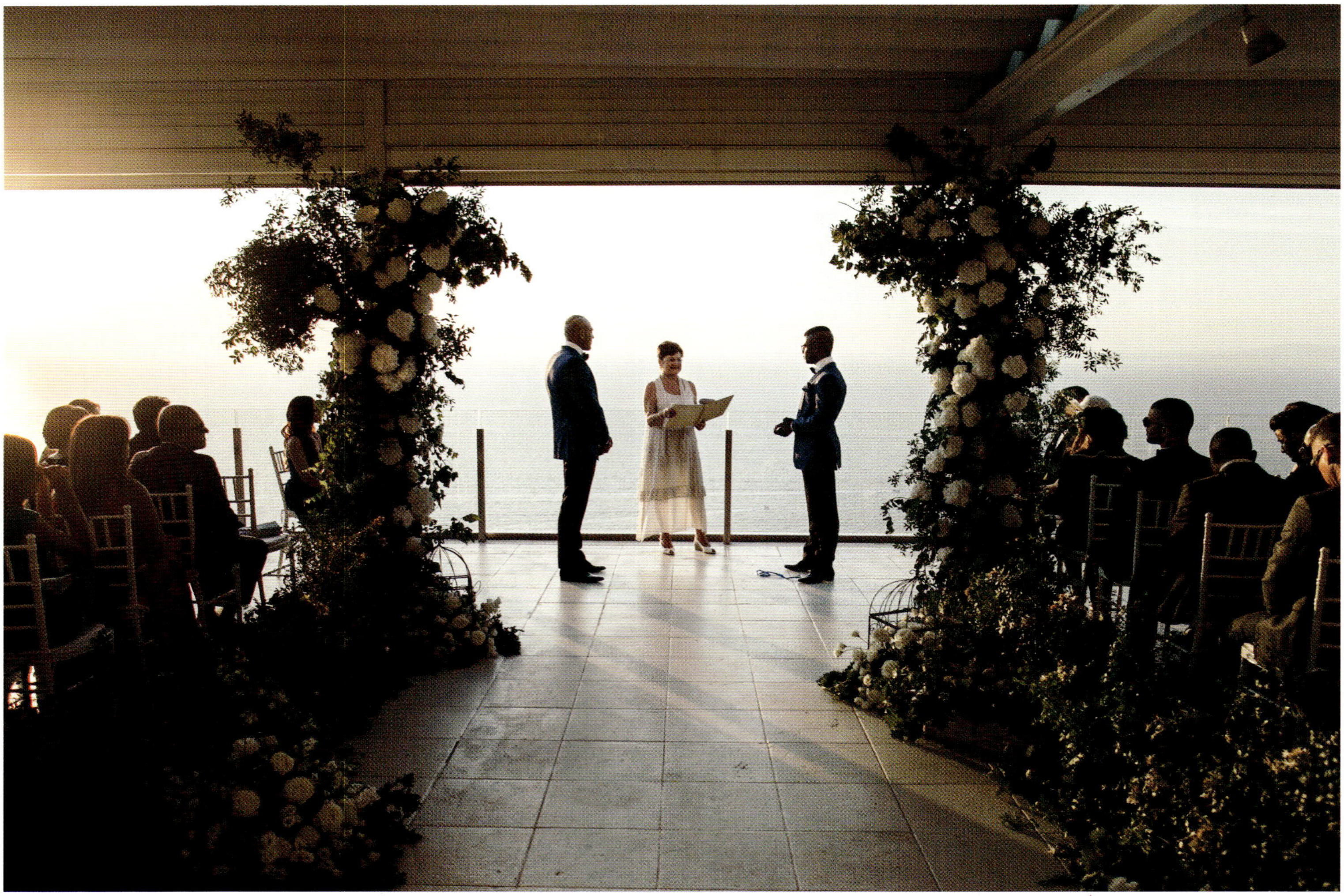

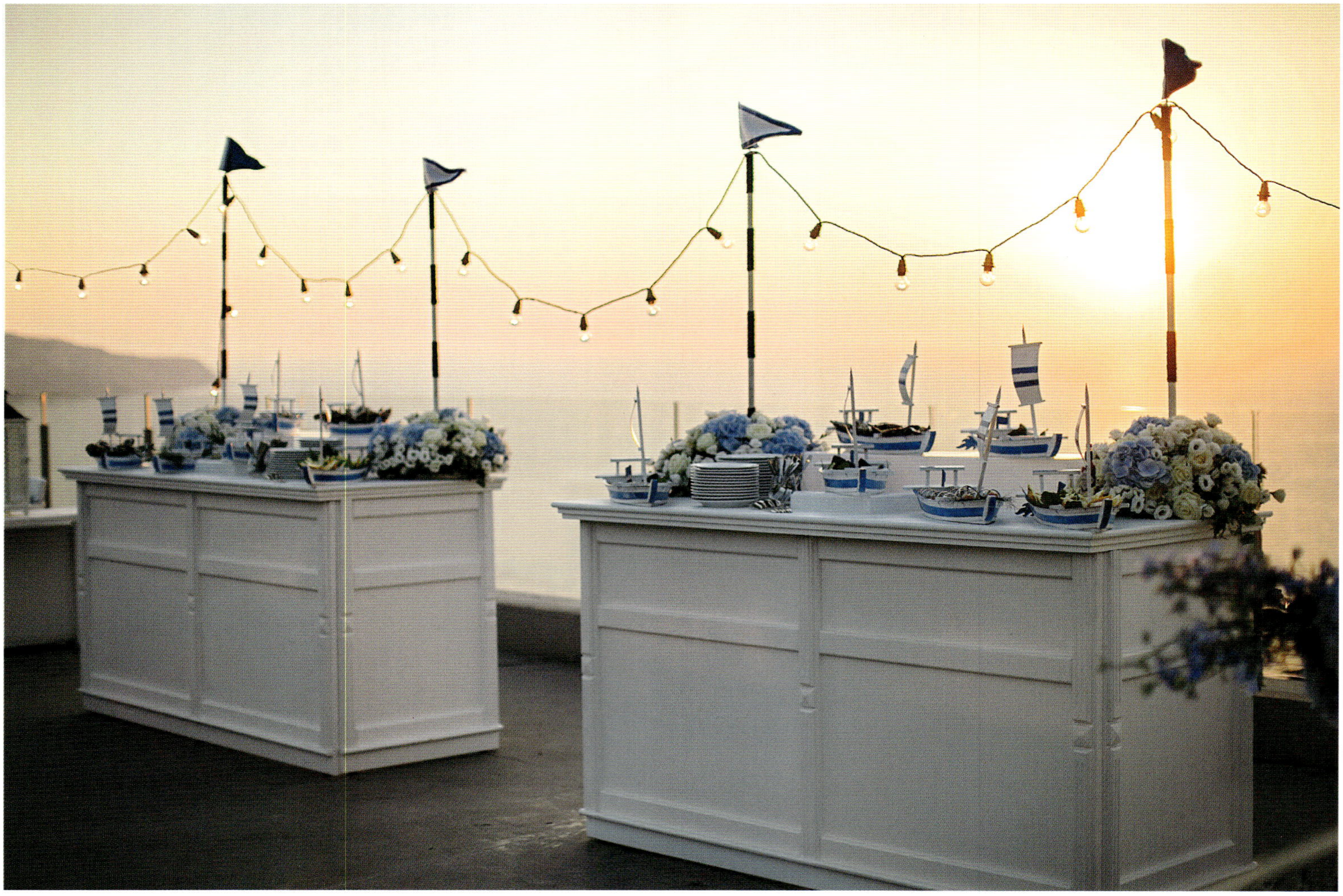

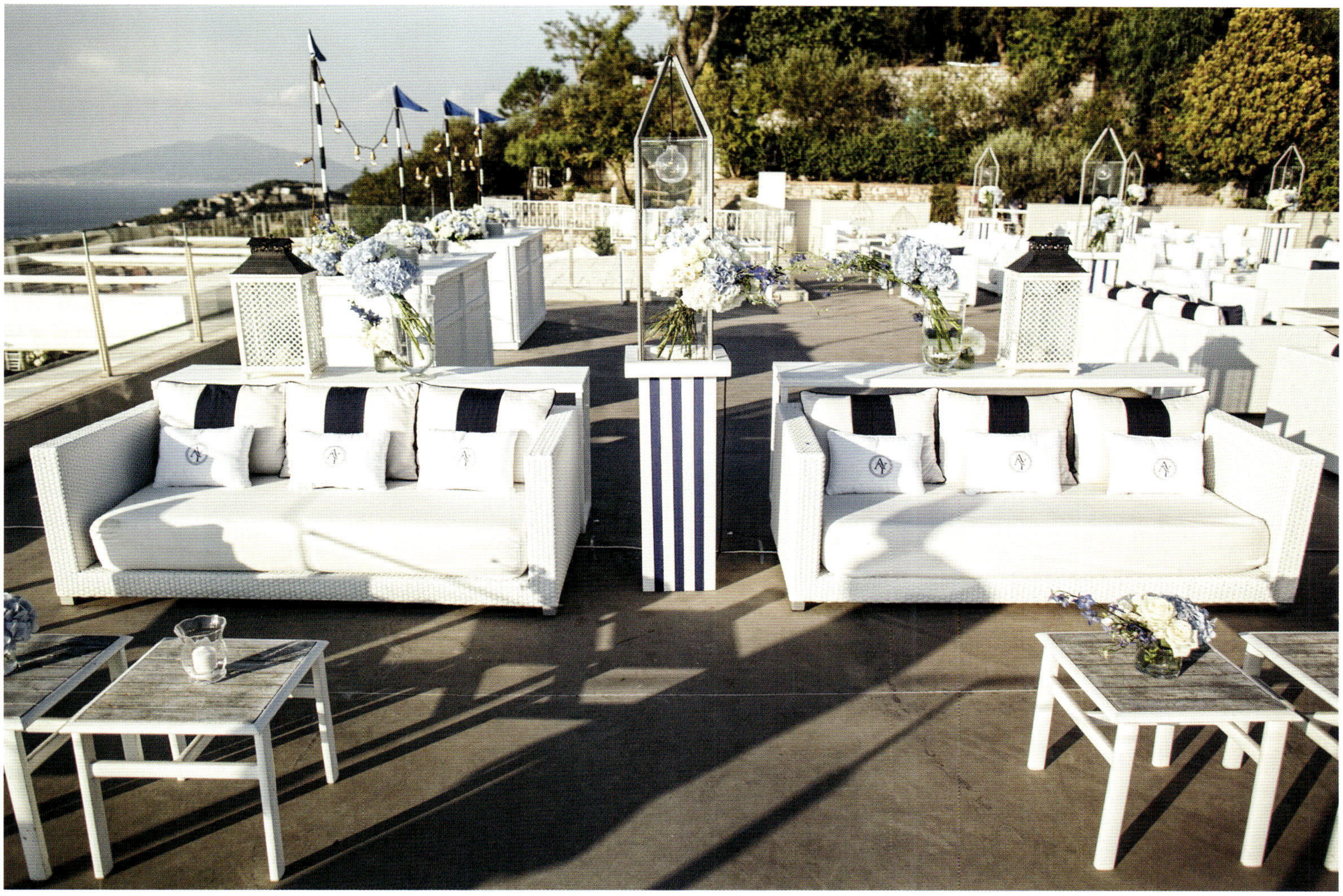

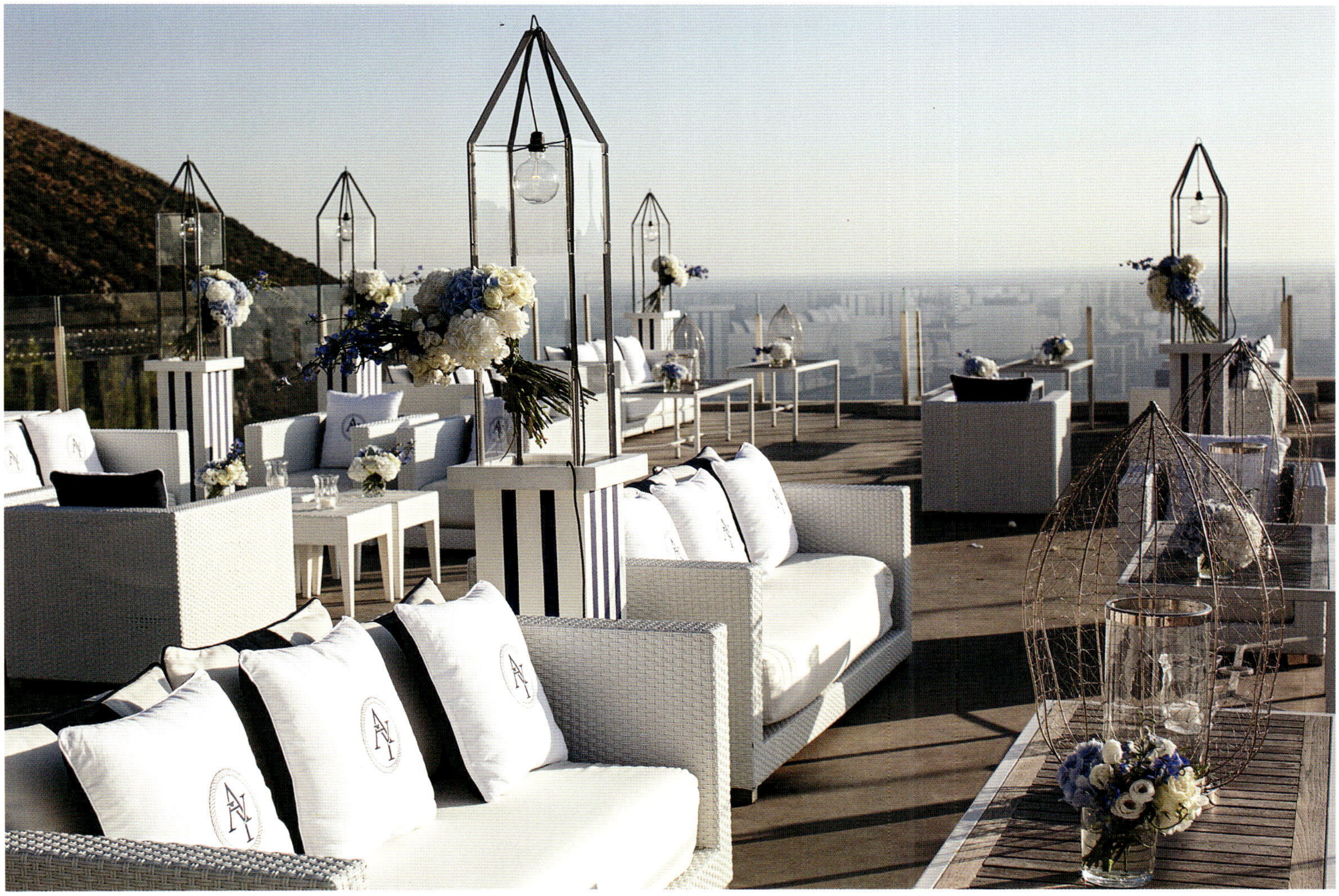

*Blue coral from the depths
of the sea decorates the tables,
and the signature color
of the event appears again
on the tablecloths, the plates
and the couples' monogram
embroidered in blue
on the napkins bound with
a sailor's knot.*

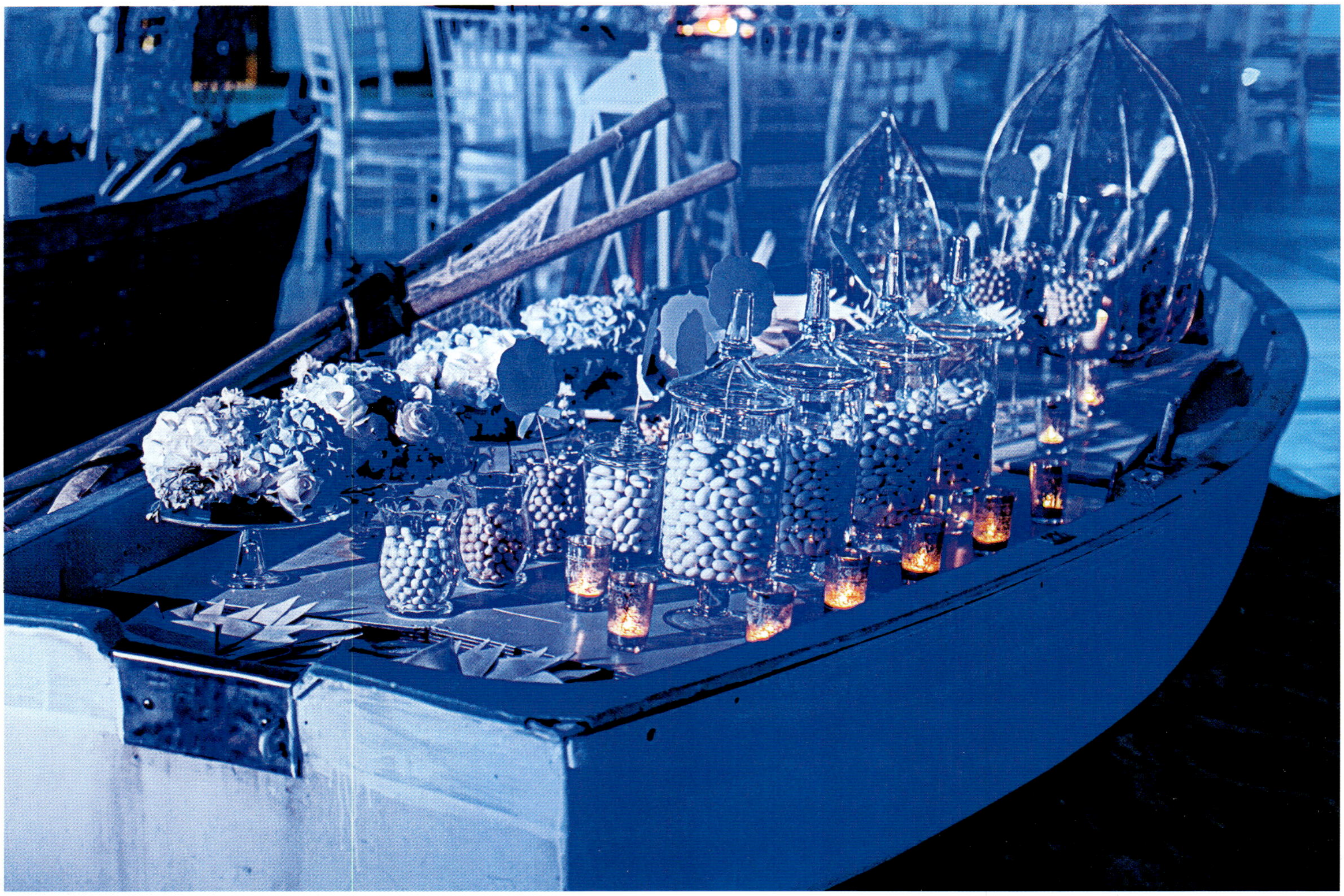

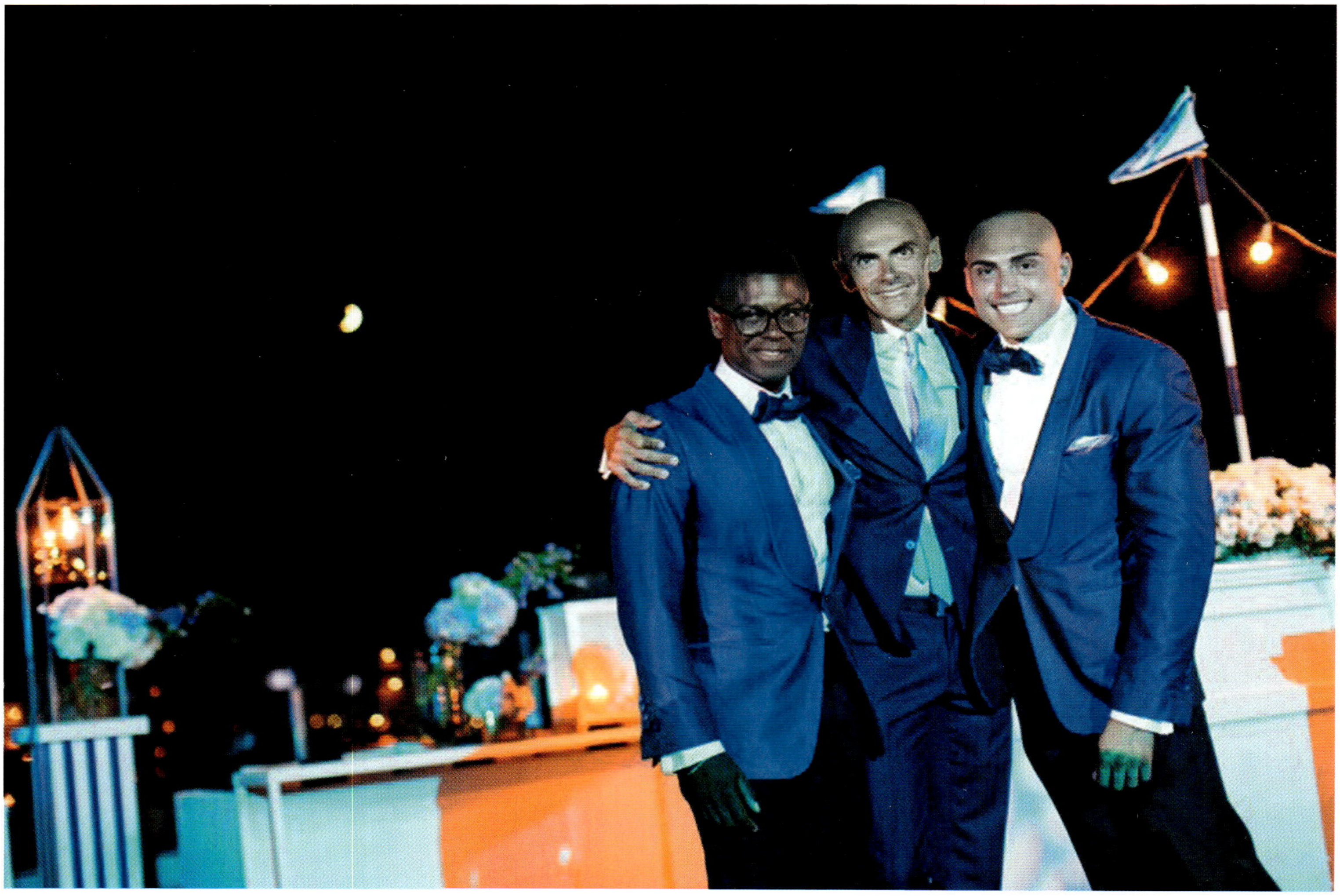

A Dream Villa

Lake Orta is generally held to be one of the most romantic scenarios in the foothills of the Alps. And it is here that Valentina and Luca have chosen to celebrate their own romance on a fine September day, although the bride arrives in a very stately Rolls Royce rather than in a carriage. She makes her way up the shallow steps to the church door on her father's arm, revealing a stunning dress of ruched ivory silk with a dramatic train. The church is decorated with dozens of bouquets of white flowers and leaves bound in trailing ribbons.

The reception is held at Villa Crespi, built by a wealthy entrepreneur determined to create a perfect Moorish palazzo on the shores of his native lake. So how to personalize a venue with such a strong identity of its own? Bespoke cut glass candelabras in a range of different sizes for a myriad of candles add an aristocratic touch to the head and satellite tables, while the gardens and walls of the villa are illuminated by a light design project encompassing creativity at its best. Hundreds of candles dotted around the lawns mark the path to the white gazebo where the cake is waiting to be cut.

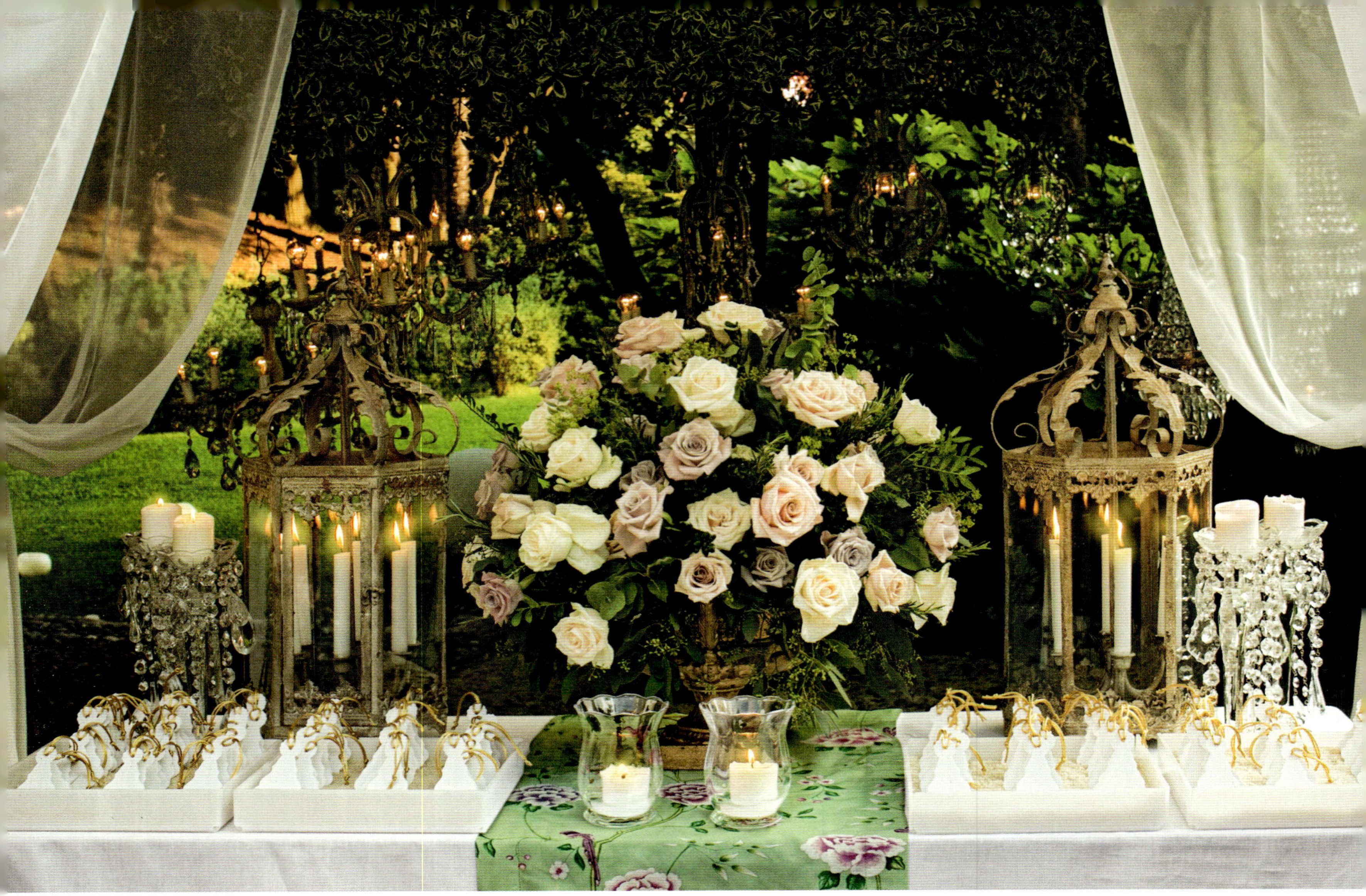

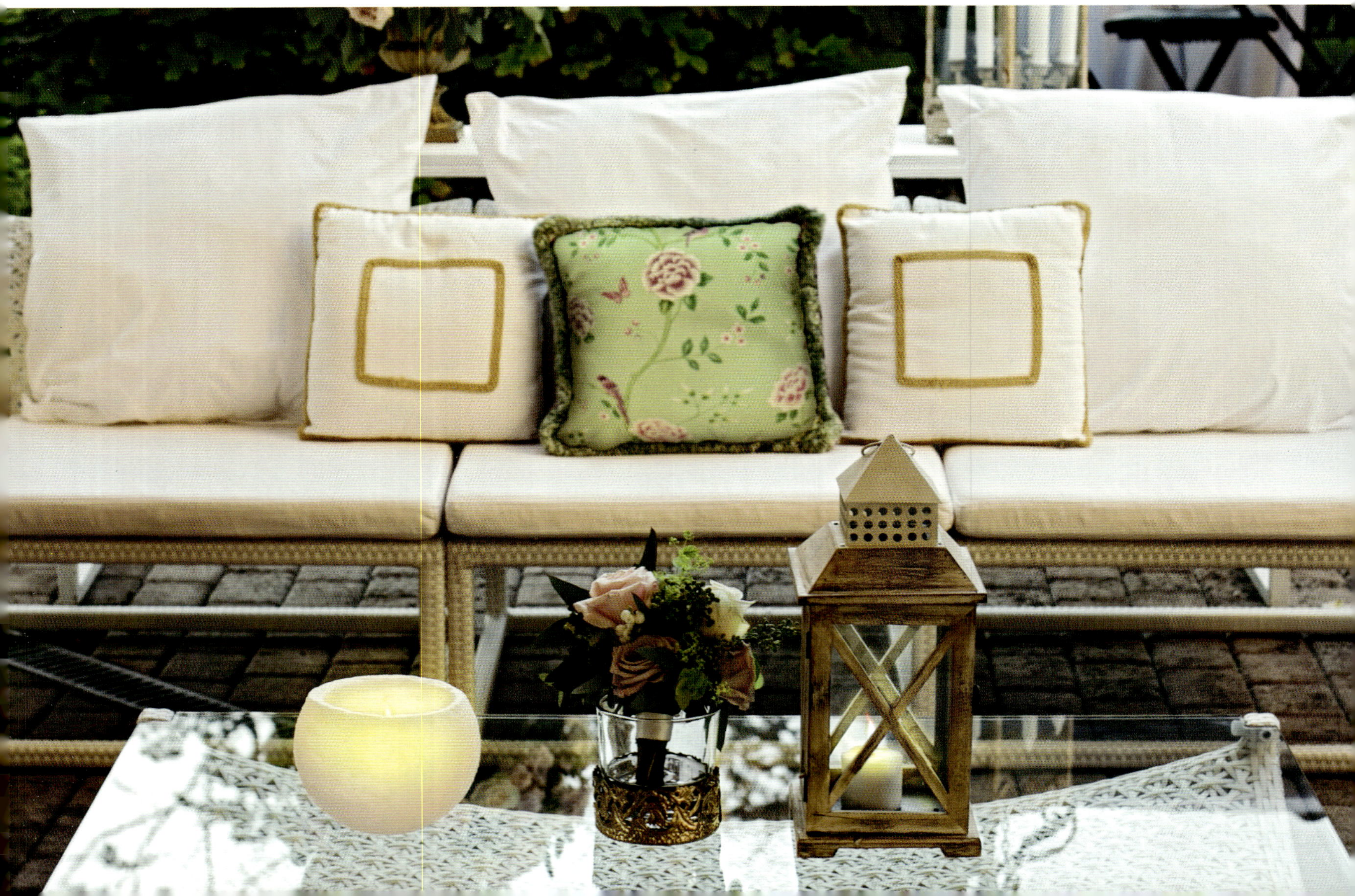

Cut glass decorations add an aristocratic touch to the illuminations, with the place cards echoing the candles scattered around the grounds of Villa Crespi. Touches of gold in the cushions and on the awnings emphasize the wealth of detail.

The bespoke cake stands were realized expressly for this occasion, rising in tiers perfect for finger food and petit fours. The traditional sugared almonds are an omen of fertility, long life, happiness and wealth.

Wedding on the Beach

Sunset on the seashore. The best possible time to get married in the opinion of Giacomo and Benedetta, a lovely couple who have decided to hold their wedding here in Forte dei Marmi in Tuscany. Neither of them are from Tuscany, but they both have fond memories of childhood holidays here by the sea, running in and out of the sea and playing hide and seek among the bathing huts that dot the shore. Which is why bathing huts feature on the "save the date" cards and are a reoccurring theme throughout the event, with bathing hut key place card holders in silver as cadeaux for the guests. The color scheme is a gaily nautical red, white and blue, with vintage wooden bathing huts constructed especially for the occasion.

The al fresco altar is framed in a very natural-looking backdrop of foliage and flowers. Elsewhere nautical references abound, from the finger food buffet served with the drinks under sunshade awnings to the wedding cake in shades of blue, decorated with little boats sailing through waves of white icing, all set on a cascade of sea foam in optic fiber.

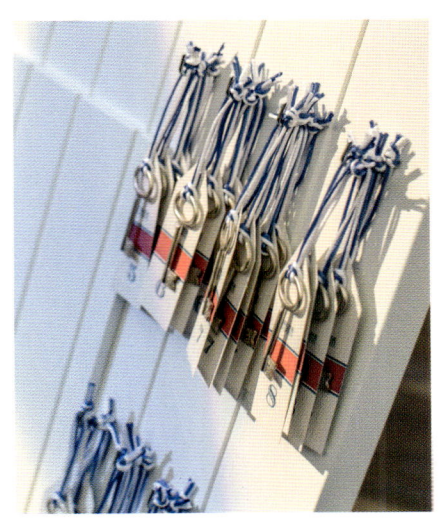

The table settings are also
a symphony of white and
shades of blue, with delicate
touches of turquoise in the
glasses and napery, while
adorable little bathing
huts in varying sizes add
a cheery note.

Tales from the East

The theme for this blessing was the mysterious East, enticingly exotic and endlessly alluring. Tents, carpets and cushions referenced a generically eastern effect free from slavish imitation, with details borrowed from a broad range of cultures. We are on the island of Capri; the bridegroom is American and the bride is from the Middle East, so as a graceful compliment to her origins we have recreated a lavish scene worthy of a *Thousand and One Nights*. The protagonist here is color. We want to achieve an atmosphere of sumptuous luxury redolent with glamour, so we have used embroidery, floral fabrics, touches of silver and gold, low tables, divans and poufs. Lanterns and hookahs complete the picture.

The table settings are more conventionally western, albeit with low divans in place of chairs, while the menu is decidedly local, the best of traditional Capri cuisine. After dinner guests are entertained with Middle Eastern music and dancing, including belly dancers flown in as a final touch.

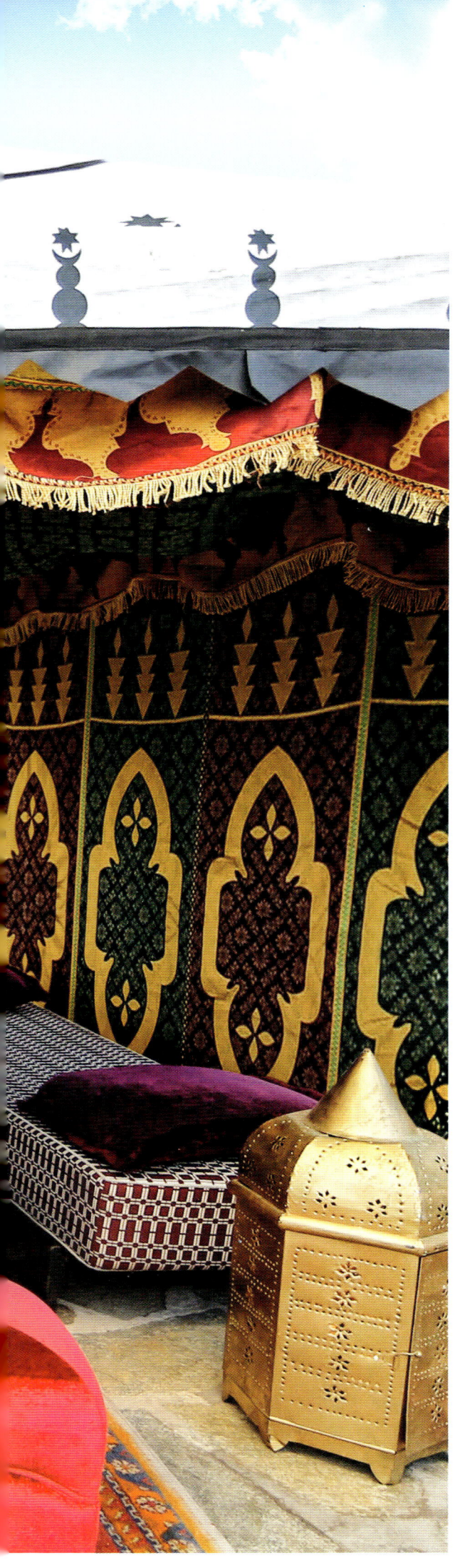

*The divans and seating
arrangements upholstered
in rich fabrics echo a Middle
Eastern home, their ample
form perfect for lounging.
Handcrafted engraved trays
do duty as coffee tables.*

*Amber, fuchsia and orange,
with hints of mother of pearl,
silver and gold all glow in
the candlelight to transform
the night into a sumptuously
enchanting wonderland.*

Bollywood Party

June, not in Rajasthan but in Italy. The bride and groom are Italian, but both have a passion for India and all things Indian, so they decide to have a traditional white church wedding and then change for an exotic evening party with their closest friends, a magnificent occasion in homage to all the elegance of the sub-continent. Starting from the perfumes: resin, sandalwood and amber...

Incense, candles and essences play a starring role in this event, an olfactory feast. The bride and her friends dazzle in brightly-colored saris and jewels fit for a maharaja as they gather in the huge gazebo decorated with flowers and lights to look like a Hindu *mandapa*, the pillared outdoor pavilion used for public rituals and weddings. The furniture and decorations are all Indian, from the poufs to the low tables, colorful cushions and carpets: a triumphal assault on the senses, with everyone joining in the dancing to the mesmerizing Indian music.

Little statues of Ganesh, the Hindu god with the head of an elephant who removes all obstacles from your path and brings luck and prosperity, are scattered around the pavilion. In the Hindu tradition Ganesh is always invoked before undertaking a new enterprise and especially on important occasions like weddings. The magic of the East seduces the guests on this early summer night.

All the colors of India: our venue has been decorated with all the colors of the rainbow, but shades of pink predominate, with touches of pink in many of the details, from the macaroons at the buffet of sweetmeats to the ribbons laced through the soft pouches with slippers provided for the ladies to take part in the dancing.

The exotic note is continued
in the decoration of the cake,
featuring Indian architecture
and elephants with raised
trunks, symbols of good luck.
The predominating pastel
shades are thrown into relief
by the gold around the base,
harbinger of wealth and
prosperity for the bridal couple.

London Celebration

Here we are in London to organize a surprise birthday party. Mission accomplished! The couple involved are old friends, and the husband has decided to organize a special celebration for his wife's fortieth birthday. It's all very hush-hush, but we find the perfect location in a deconsecrated church in Mayfair, transformed for the occasion into the legendary Studio 54, the Manhattan disco famous for its original artistic performances and its extravaganza evenings.

The aisle has been turned into a huge illuminated dance floor where the guests from Italy can all boogie the night away, in a kaleidoscope of light design, video installations and lashing of seventies sounds mixed by Kenny Carpenter, the famous Studio 54 DJ, installed in a transparent bubble 8 meters above the dance floor. Professional dancers in vintage seventies gear take to the floor for some of the most famous numbers, and the "cake" makes its virtual appearance on a LED wall, while waiters distribute portions of real cake to the guests.

Happy birthday, my darling!

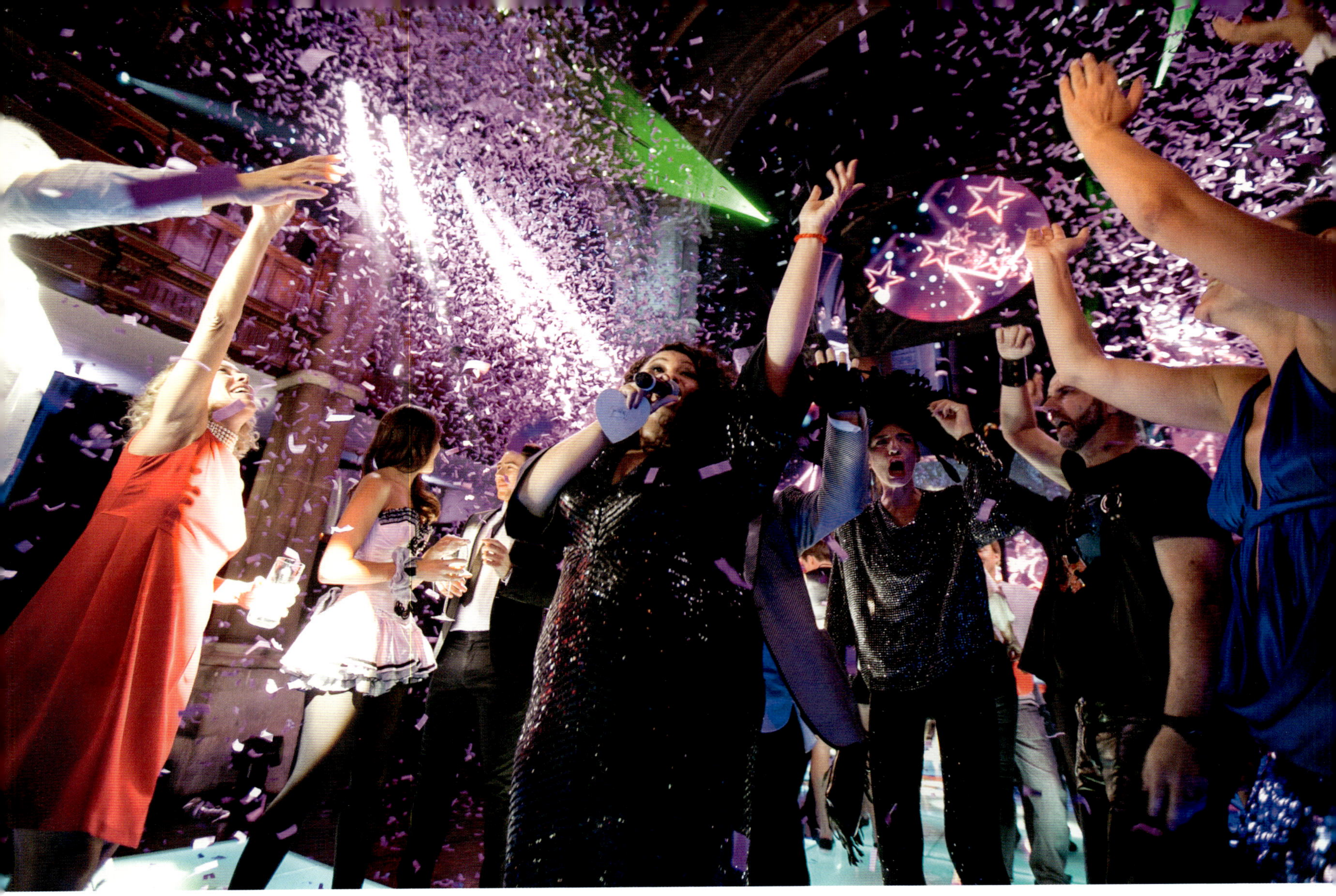

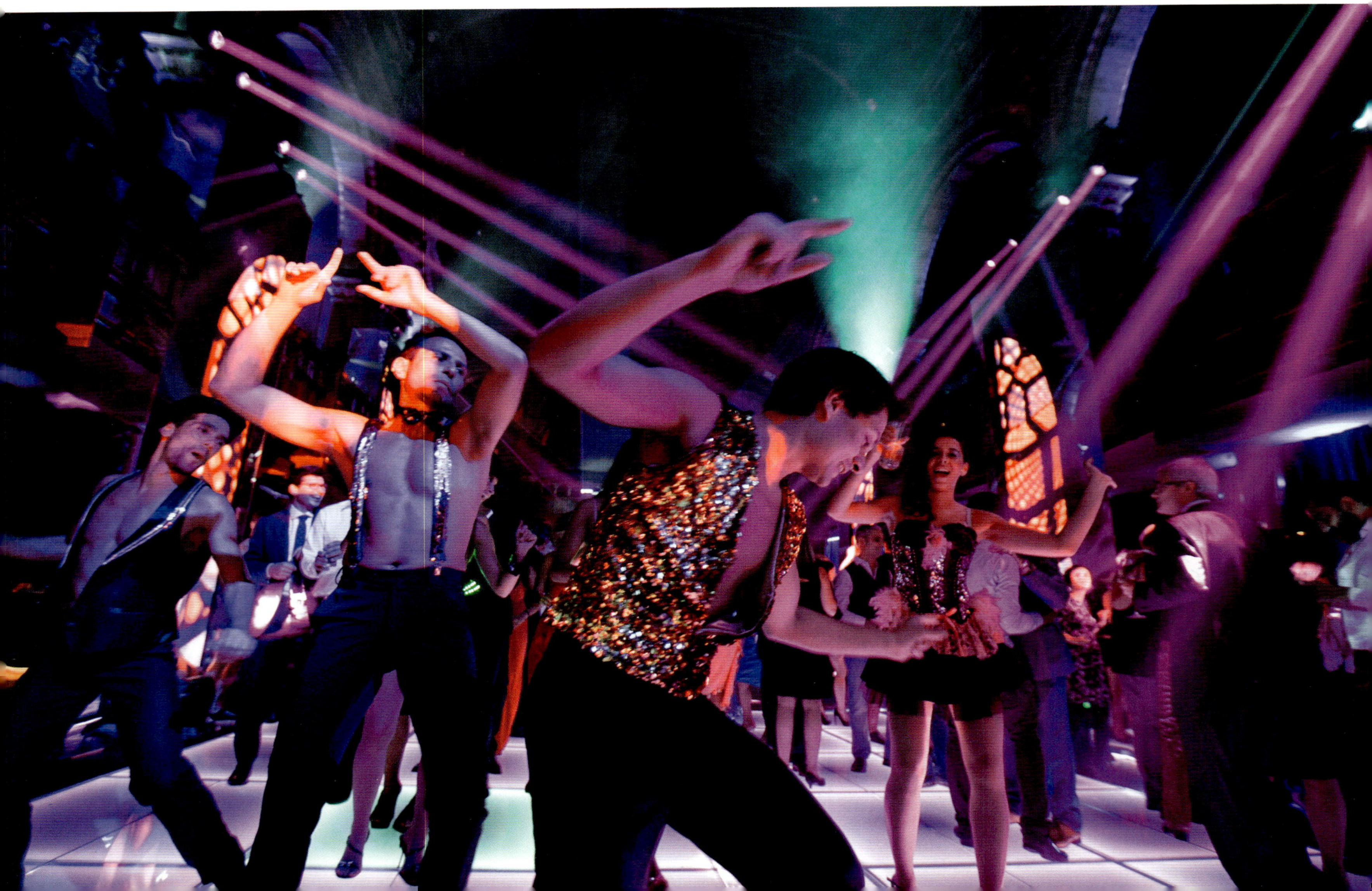

Acknowledgements

To stage all my events in Italy and around the world I rely on a team of top professionals. So I would like to thank them for all their hard work, dedication and untiring devotion in providing support for every wonderful new adventure.

Thank you Riccardo, Sara, Carolina, Roberta, Giuseppe and all the craftsmen, technicians, workers, warehouse staff and drivers who transform each new project into concrete reality.

Photo Credits
Joanne Dunn: p. 223
Raoul Iacometti: pp. 84-95, 221, 223
Alfonso Longobardi: pp. 104-113, 220
Luca Rajna: p. 222
Enzo Recchia: pp. 202-211, 220
Studio Fotografico Migliaccio: pp. 194-201
Studio Fotografico Ruggiero Farina: p. 220
Studio Morlotti: cover, pp. 6, 20-31, 32-41, 42-51, 52-63, 65, 66-73, 74-83, 96-103, 114-125, 126-139, 140-151, 152-161, 162-169, 170-183, 184-193, 212, 213-217, 220, 221, 222, 223
Studio Magmatika: pp. 8-19, 65, 66, 220

Graphic Design
Anna Piccarreta - arachidepiù

Texts by
Lucia Moretti

Translation by
Studio Queens srl (Milan), Sarah Wood

Distributed in English throughout the World
by Rizzoli International Publications Inc.
300 Park Avenue South
New York, NY 10010, USA

ISO 9001
Mondadori Electa S.p.A. is certified for the Quality Management System
by Bureau Veritas Italia S.p.A., in compliance with UNI EN ISO 9001:2008.

This book respects the environment
The paper used was produced using wood from forests managed
to strict environmental standards; the companies involved guarantee
sustainable production certified environmentally.

This volume was printed for Mondadori Electa S.p.A.
at Elcograf S.p.A., via Mondadori 15, Verona
Printed in Italy